FIRST
GENERATION

Stories of Rebels and Pioneers

RICK & BEV ZACHARY

Bonhoeffer Publishing

Copyright © 2017 Bonhoeffer Publishing

Illustrations by Anna Ruda

All rights reserved

Cataloging-in-Publication Data on file

Library of Congress

ISBN: 978-0-9899692-9-1

Printed In the United States

www.bonhoefferpublishing.com

TABLE OF CONTENTS

To Rosanie

He shows mercy
from generation to generation
to all who fear him.
Luke 1:50 NLT

INTRODUCTION

Rick

A few years ago, I sat cross-legged on a mat in a mud-floor home and taught a group of Tharu believers. The Tharu are an ancient people who still live much like their ancestors lived over a thousand years ago. Their primitive villages straddle the border between Nepal and India, and their rice fields grace the low-lying plains. These days they travel in buses to the city markets. They have electricity and ride bicycles, with a mobile phone perched between their ears and shoulders. Oftentimes a satellite dish sits outside their home, tethered to a solar-powered television that sits in a mud wall's molded niche. Some of their homes are entirely solar powered, and a few of them use clever underground biogas processing systems that convert animal dung into methane for cooking. But they are still connected to the land they farm in an almost mystical way.

In their homes almost everything you touch is crafted from the materials they find nearby. The bed frame is hand hewn from forest timber, the careful machete marks smoothed by years of use. The taut mat support is handwoven from sisal or grass gathered from plants in the nearby jungle. They form their houses from the earth, the thick exterior mud walls stained with the ochre pigment of a jungle plant. Large pottery vessels hold their stores of grain, drinking water, and buffalo milk. They coat their earthen, thatch-shaded porches every morning with a glaze of mud mixed with cow dung.[1]

Hand-forged tools lean against the wall near the door: a hoe, an axe, a heavy digging rod. Village blacksmiths fashion most of the tools, beating metal from old car and truck frames into useful shapes. The hardwood handles are dark and waxy from years of rough-palmed chafing. There are only a few market-purchased items in their homes: a machete, some cooking pots, a packet of sewing needles, a bolt of cloth. Everything else is hacked from the earth and the forest.

When they move or die, their homes disinte-grate without a trace back into the earth. The jungle reclaims the land, and within a decade there is no trace that they were ever there. Their ancient organic soil, farmed for three thousand years, renews every season under their management. They waste nothing.

When the Tharu pray, they weep fat tears that dampen the packed dirt floors of their homes. They wail and lament, their sorrow rising in a keening chorus. I never liked it. I've tried to teach them about grace and joy, but they always return to their intense, mournful prayers.

I've witnessed that same behavior in other developing world cultures: among Latin American

Indians, Africans, Indonesians, Pakistanis, and indigenous tribes across India and Asia. I've tried unsuccessfully to change it.

But on that evening, sitting on the floor with the men, it occurred to me that perhaps they were in touch with things I could not comprehend. I noticed their calloused, soil-stained feet tucked beneath them. I watched them beat their chests with roughened hands, their nails blackened with the earth. I could smell the sweet hint of curry that seeped from their pores with their sweat and dampened their stained shirts. These people were far removed from the grid I depended on. They were connected to the earth in a way that I would never comprehend.

Perhaps, I thought, they understand what the scripture means that says, "For we know that all creation has been groaning as in the pains of childbirth right up to the present time. And we believers also groan, even though we have the Holy Spirit within us as a foretaste of future glory, for we long for our bodies to be released from sin and suffering" (Romans 8:22–23 NLT).

Perhaps these primitive believers, many of them illiterate, can sense something that we cannot. Perhaps they hear a groaning that we cannot hear in our sterile, synthetic, self-absorbed world. Perhaps they can teach us something about faith and love and living.

These Nepali Christians may be some of the best examples we have of the early church. They are first-generation believers. Their theology is uncomplicated, their faith is innocent, and their lives are pure. We rarely hear their stories told in their voices. I've tried to do that here with selections from the low-plains tribes near India to the mountain people near the China border. I hope their stories touch your life in the same way they have touched mine.

*"I am giving you a sign
of my covenant with you
and with all living creatures,
for all generations to come."*
Genesis 9:12 NLT

INDRADREV

Rick

In our first venture into west Nepal, Bev and I spent three months in Nepalgunj, visiting villages and dreaming together with KB and Sushila Basel[2] about the work before us. My first meeting was a three-day event with eighteen young pastors. They were not really pastors. Most of them were teenagers, the youngest sixteen. They were village boys with primary educations, and they had known the Lord for less than a year. But they were smart and earnest, and all we had, so we called them leaders and pastors.

I sat cross-legged on the floor with those boys and taught them for three days, from early morning until evening. They took notes and asked questions. I remember praying over them at the end of those three days and speaking by faith over each one of them. We released them to return to their villages and start churches.

About six months later, we gathered again for three more days of ministry. They shared amazing reports of growing congregations, healing miracles, grace through persecutions, and financial provision. Two visiting pastors from America were with me, sharing the ministry time. At the close of those three days, we washed those young teenaged pastors' feet.

I have a vivid memory of kneeling before each of them, their tears splashing onto the back of my head as I looked at their brown, calloused, rice-farmer feet. I remember marveling over them. They were teenagers, nearly every one of them, and yet we were witnessing the beginning of something spectacular. I knew then that I was seeing something I had never seen in my lifetime and may never see again—the beginning of a movement.

One of those young men was Indradrev.

So those who are last now
will be first then,
and those who are first will be last
Matthew 20:16 NLT

He was a quiet, gentle man, a tent dweller—more a Jacob than an Esau,[3] but despite his unassuming ways, he was a warrior. Sometimes heroes are obvious. Like David or Abraham or Moses, they tower over the rest of us: ruddy, handsome, fearless, charismatic. And sometimes we don't know a man is a hero until a crisis outs him. Sometimes men rise out of anonymity to surprise us all.

The heroes living among us in obscurity eventually have their moment, and when it happens, they don't realize how audacious they are. They do things that most of us only dream of doing. Like a still-water stretch in a river, they are not yet fathomed. They are ordinary, unsung, and unappreciated; and in their moment, we are surprised. They are not. They say, "I just did what anyone would have done."

He was sixteen, with sloping shoulders and a pleasant, unassuming smile, but within him was a legend. He could see things that others could not see, and he had dreams that others dared not dream. He knew there was a better path, but he did not know where that path was or where to begin looking for it. When he heard of the Christians, he was curious. When he visited their place of worship, he was convinced. When he saw he could become one of them, he joined, and when he joined, something changed within. Somehow, in a quiet act of submission to this new King, he felt as if he had been knighted. Like his ancestors, the renowned Gurkha[4] warriors, he arose from that tear-stained altar a man.

His father was not impressed. He shouted, he railed, and he threatened to beat him, but the boy stood firm. Before his seventeenth birthday, he started a church. He built a little hut on the corner of his family land, and he started meeting on Saturday mornings with a group of six boys—his teenaged disciples.

A woman in Majhgaun was dying. She heard

that the Christians could heal the sick, so she sent word to Indradrev to come and pray for her. She had been ill for three years and had gone to India for treatment. They had told her she had cancer, given her six months to live, and sent her back to her village. She had returned to Majhgaun, where she withered away. She lay in the dark, her sunken face drawn tight against her skull, exposing the hideous stained teeth, the receding gums, and the hollow, empty eyes.

Her granddaughter, a timid little girl, visited Indradrev and asked him to come and pray for her grandmother. In his devotion that morning, he had read: "Are any of you sick? You should call for the elders of the church to come and pray over you, anointing you with oil in the name of the Lord. Such a prayer offered in faith will heal the sick, and the Lord will make you well. And if you have committed any sins, you will be forgiven" (James 5:14–15 NLT).

His elders were sixteen and fifteen-year-old boys. But he called them to go with him, and they prayed for the stricken old woman. They prayed in trembling teenaged voices, their eyes clenched tight against the frail horror that lay on that piteous cot. Nothing happened.

The next day the little granddaughter returned. She was not as timid as the day before. "Grandmamma is better today. She cooked eggs for us, and she ate a chapatti."

And on that day, his unassuming legend began. Over the next few months, the old woman recovered. No one could silence her. She became a village crier for the modest young pastor who had built a little church of mud and sticks on the edge of his father's garden. By the time he was eighteen, his church members were crowded around the outside of his ramshackle building, seventy-five strong, and unable to fit into the tiny mud house.

His father continued to rail.

At nineteen he built his second building, a much more substantial structure. His congregation, no longer intimidated by the villagers' threats, had become a force in the region. The Maoists noticed. They were hungry for rising young leaders, and they were accustomed to having their way. They recruited with flattery and promises and a grand benevolence that everyone knew could not be refused. If the Maoists wanted them, there was no choice but to join. They asked him to become one of them.

Indradrev refused.

The rebels came while he was praying in the church. He took hold of one of the church pillars when they tried to drag him away, and for a while they could not pry him off. But they were many, and eventually he tired. They took him into the jungle to meet their leader.

"We've noticed you," the commander said.

He did not answer.

"You will be one of our top leaders. We will make you the leader of not only your village, but also your region. This is a great opportunity. Very few of our leaders are as young as you. You have potential, and you will rise quickly in our ranks. You should not turn this down."

The commander sat on the edge of a makeshift campstool, leaning toward him, intense, intimidating, and insistent. He was a large man, seasoned from years of living on the edge of civilization, hardened from battles with the Nepali police and military, lean from the simple insurgent diet and constant moving about. He was not accustomed to teenaged boys refusing him.

"I am happy with what I am doing," Indradrev said. "I want to serve the Lord."

The commander reasoned with him for over an hour, but the boy would not budge. Finally, he said, "If you don't join us, we will kill you."

"I am ready to die. I will not join your movement." He looked directly into the commander's eyes and, through a long silence, held an unwavering, steady gaze. Both the man and the boy were determined. But the commander had more to lose in this conflict of wills. His men stood nearby. They were watching.

"I think you are mentally disturbed," the Maoist finally said. "I'm not going to punish you today. I'm going to give you some time to think about our conversation. After you've reconsidered, I'll visit you again and we will continue this discussion."

When they came the second time, the church was in the middle of a service. They were praying, and Indradrev, with his eyes closed, had a peculiar feeling that something was wrong. He opened his eyes and saw the Maoist commander entering the back door of the church. Indradrev ran to him before he could fully enter the building.

"How are you, brother?" Indradrev asked.

"You disobedient dog! Did I not tell you not to meet in this building?" The commander glared down at him, red-faced, clenching his fists. Just outside the building, his men stood ready, their AKs unslung. The Maoist leader wore a pistol on his hip, the black leather military holster unsnapped and partially open.

Indradrev stood before him, holding his gaze. He was not confrontational, but neither was he fearful. Rather than lowering his eyes, he looked directly at the commander, hoping his look appeared gracious. He was about to speak and tell the man they were harmless people and not political. They wanted to live simple lives and help one another.

As he opened his mouth to speak, the commander moved forward, his twisting torso leveraging his weight behind a right cross that caught Indradrev just below the eye. The commander's ring split the skin over Indradrev's cheekbone, and the blood poured.

One of the men in the congregation stood and

said, "Please, don't do this. We are not harming anyone here. We don't want any trouble. My wife was healed through this young man's prayer, and many others here have been healed. We have seen the power and the blessing. That is why we are following him."

The commander watched through narrowing eyes while the man spoke; then, without warning, he struck the man. When the Christian fell, the commander kneeled on his chest and continued to beat him. By the third blow, the believer was unconscious.

The rebel leader stood before the trembling congregation and shouted, "If you gather here again, we will bomb this church. We will comb through this village, and we will find each of your homes. We will kill you, and we will take your children with us."

The Maoists left without another word, and the intimidated church members dispersed. That evening some of the men met to discuss what they should do. Indradrev remembered the stories of the persecuted Chinese believers, how they divided themselves into small groups and met quietly in their homes. He told his men, "We will do the same. We will go underground." For more than six months, the church met secretly in homes.

The house meetings caused the church to grow even faster. There were many miracles, and though the villagers were afraid, they continued to join with the Christians. Six months passed, and it seemed to all the believers that the Maoists had decided to leave them alone. They held a prayer meeting without incident on Good Friday and decided that night to hold an Easter service.

Easter was a beautiful morning, a little hot, but fresh and clear. Indradrev was standing under a lemon tree when they came. Someone had just given him a steaming cup of tea and a sweet biscuit. There was a stir outside the wall of hedges that surrounded the church compound, and an unruly group of men entered, all of them armed.

One of them shouted, "Who is Indradrev?"

Indradrev did not want to endanger his congregation, so he stepped forward from under the tree. "I am," he said simply.

They took him to the commander, who was visiting a nearby home. When he saw Indradrev, he shouted, "What kind of foolish animal are you?"

"Bring a rope and tie him up," he ordered his men. "We will take him into the mountains and shoot him there."

A large crowd of villagers had gathered, and they stood in silence. All of them thought Indradrev would die. He thought, too, that he would die, but with all the village watching, he spoke calmly to the commander. "Why don't you come and join us for our festival? We've slaughtered a goat, and all the women brought food from their homes. Bring your men and we'll feast together."

The commander was trapped. If he accepted

Indradrev's invitation, he would appear weak. If he killed a hospitable man, he would insult the age-old traditions. The Christians had grown in number. They would spread the word of whatever happened today across the region. He could lose much of the political influence he had fought to gain. He thought for a moment and said, "Thank you for your invitation, but we will not be joining you." The two men shook hands, and the Maoists retreated to their jungle stronghold.

The believers in Majhgaun went back underground. They used the church occasionally. Indradrev sealed and locked the front door of the building, but sometimes, in the evenings or early mornings, small groups would meet there for prayer. They came silently, one by one through the side door, and their prayers within the building were like the hushed stir of early morning.

Good buildings in the villages are rare, and the Christians' churches were by far the largest and most well constructed in the region. Once the Maoists established themselves, they were emboldened. No longer fearing the Nepali military, they came out of their jungle hideouts and lived openly in the villages. They seized Indradrev's building and set up their headquarters in the church.

The commander and many of his men slept in the church, so Indradrev began sleeping there with them, hoping to influence the commander. Long conversations evolved between the two men, one reasoning through political ideology, the other with spiritual sensibility. They became friends.

They never resolved their differences. The commander never accepted the gospel, but after about three months, he asked Indradrev to sit with him.

"I know you are not happy that we are living here in your building," he said. "I have decided not to use it any longer. We are moving to another location."

And that was the end of the Maoist uprising in Majhgaun. They came with intimidation, and anger, and threats. They left as humble as lambs—their bluster spent, their ideology fruitless, their revolution parried by a twenty-year-old, slope-shouldered shepherd boy.[5]

*"This is my eternal name,
my name to remember
for all generations."*
Exodus 3:15 NLT

SUSHILA

Bev

In the early 1990s, Nepal opened to the gospel. At that time, the king of Nepal[6] was honored as if he were a god. There were few churches, and believers were persecuted. Nepal was the world's only Hindu kingdom, and Christianity had never been permitted. With the democracy movement of the nineties, there was an explosion of churches across the central and eastern regions. Western Nepal, however, remained largely untouched.

In the midnineties, a powerful Maoist[7] insurgency formed. They were especially strong in the west. That uprising was the beginning of the end for the Hindu kingdom. Violence and political instability made evangelism and the growth of the gospel very difficult, but still, in the central region and in the east, the gospel advanced.

In 2007 everything changed when the Maoists agreed to turn their armaments over to the United Nations, and the UN cached them in a huge depot in the northwestern mountains. In 2008 the Maoists gained representation in the Nepali parliament. I thought it would embolden the Communists and make our task even more difficult, but the opposite happened. In order to form a working coalition, the Maoists cooperated with rival political parties and, among other things, relaxed their opposition to the Christian movements. They worked to form a secular democracy, which eventually opened the nation's west to development and socioeconomic change.

When I traveled to the remote areas during that time, I often passed through Maoist-controlled territory. The hammer and sickle of the Communist Party was stenciled in blood red on buildings, bridge abutments, and homes all across the country, especially in the outlying regions. Young boys and girls, barely in their teens, were forcibly drafted out of the villages and into the rebel army, where they were indoctrinated in the Maoists' radical version of Communism. They lived in isolated communal camps and were courageous guerilla fighters. The Nepali army feared their attacks.

Maoist thugs intimidated shopkeepers in the small towns and cities across the west, demanding support for their cause. There were bombings and ferocious attacks on army installations, and the Nepali army initiated counterattacks against the Maoist strongholds. The Nepalis were caught in the crossfire between the warring factions, and as in most insurgencies, the innocent suffered most of all. Across the country there were food and fuel shortages, electrical-grid disruptions, dangerous political rallies, work strikes, and general confusion.

It was about this time that we met KB and Sushila Basel. Over the next ten years, we would experience a rare privilege—we witnessed a movement. There are few places remaining on earth where there is not some representation of the gospel. There are many places that are unreached, but there are few that are untouched. West Nepal in the early 2000s was untouched.

The growth we saw in those early days was unprecedented, and our tendency was to attribute that growth to the leadership principles and organic growth strategies we were teaching. But later we began to understand the powerful spiritual engine that was an important part of the ministry's rapid growth: Sushila's energetic prayer ministry and fearless works of compassion.

She opens her arms to the poor and
extends her hands to the needy . . .
She is clothed with strength . . .
she can laugh at the days to come.
Proverbs 31:20, 25 NIV

Sushila has a husky laugh. It has a round, rich quality, like a bell, but not in the way fairy tales describe a feminine laugh—a tinkling, delightful sound. No, her laugh is deep and resounding, like an iron bell from an old, buttressed cathedral.

And her voice does the same thing as a cathedral's bells—it calls people to reverence. She is powerful.

This morning we are standing on her porch. She is holding a baby in her arms. Sushila is a grandmother already, but she's taken in another child to raise as a daughter. The baby's biological mother was about to crush her with a rock when a church member stopped her and brought the infant to Sushila. The baby was starved to the point of organ failure and had to spend a month in neonatal intensive care. This morning she is four months old and is braced in Sushila's arms, held tight against her chest. She grins as Sushila's laugh shakes her.

Sushila is looking beyond me, over the balcony of the porch. Near the large gate to her house, there is an old, saggy, naked woman. The woman's face is so crinkled and drooped I wonder if she can see, and when she smiles up at us, her one tooth shows. Draped skin covers most of her body parts, and she looks more like a caricature than an object of scandal. She bows to us—the formal Christian Nepali greeting. "She is making me mad!" Sushila says. But she doesn't look mad; she looks amused. "She is always throwing her dress somewhere."

Eventually fully clothed, the woman sits next to her housemates, two old ladies who live on the compound. They each have a plate of steaming *dal bhat*[8] they swish in circles with their fingers. At random intervals, each stuffs a handful of food into their mouth and chews slowly. They don't speak or connect with one another. They just stare ahead, like a tired child at dinner.

There is a short, heavy lady in the bunch. A family member had brought her as a visitor to KB and Sushila's church. That day Laxmi wore a small strip of fabric as a miniskirt, but was topless. Her hair was a spiky shock of white, shooting up from her skeletal alien features, and she carried a large walking stick. Randomly, throughout the service, she would bop people on the head with the stick. Everyone excused her because she was obviously mentally unstable. When the service ended, the crowd dwindled, and even the woman who had brought her disappeared. But the lady remained, and she's lived with Sushila and KB ever since.

Over time, she regained her senses and told them her story. Laxmi was married before, but when she had her mental breakdown, her husband lost his patience and tied a rope around her neck, dragging her to the jungle where he abandoned her.

Sometimes, these days, she sneaks out of the house gates and plucks branches from trees and sticks them in her hair to perform a tribal dance in the middle of the highway, but KB and Sushila always find her and bring her back home.

One of the ladies sitting in the group is taller than the others—Nirmala. As I watch them, Nirmala makes eye contact with me and holds it for long enough that I know she is in her right mind at the moment. Sometimes she is sane, every fifteen days to be exact. She's done that for more than a decade.

The third woman, Kausila, Sushila found on the streets. Every day Sushila saw her on the road, digging through garbage. One day she approached the homeless woman. "Where is your house? Would you like to come home with me?" Sushila asked.

Kausila looked up. "Food?"

Sushila helped the woman walk home with her. Once they arrived, Sushila bathed her and cut her hair and scrubbed her head, removing lice and remnants of dreadlocks. She clipped her nails and cleaned under them and gave her new clothes to wear. Then they sat and ate together. Sushila and KB's home at the time was a one-room church building where their two sons and the two other women lived with them. But the family had more than the women did, so they shared with them.

A few years after Kausila came to live with them, a new church member identified her as their aunt. They were able to tell Sushila and KB Kausila's story. Many years before, someone had trafficked her across the border to India and sold her to a Muslim man. She lived with him for years as his house slave. He raped her repeatedly and she had a son.

The man didn't like how much Kausila loved her child; he thought she gave the boy too much attention and was distracted from her housework. He took Kausila and their son to the nearby track, and as a train approached, he threw their son in front of it. Kausila watched the churning wheels crush her baby. In that moment, she broke. Her master had no use for a crazy woman, so he turned Kausila out into the streets. She made her way back to the Nepali border, and into Sushila and KB's city. Kausila had lost the only hope she had—a baby in the midst of her slavery. Over the years, she has gained back pieces of her memory and sanity. But time can never heal what she has experienced.

I watch the three women eat their lunch, and I think of the amount of wisdom lost. They should be surrounded by their grandbabies, bossing a daughter-in-law around, feeding an old husband dal bhat. Instead, they dawdle around like children, urinating outside, chasing chickens, and being dressed and redressed by loving caretakers and church members. They are deeply loved by their new family. They would have no chance of survival on their own, and in Nepal there is not a health system in place to support them.

Sushila isn't an idle woman. Any need she sees, she figures out a way to fill it. Some bring stray kittens home; she brings stray people home. The need overwhelms most, but it fuels Sushila and KB.

Five years ago they heard statistics about their city, Nepalgunj. The number of people trafficked from Nepal into India was astounding. At that time, the Global Slavery Index ranked Nepal as having the fifth-highest number of enslaved people in the world. Since then, the statistics for Nepal have improved but slavery is still estimated to be a $32 billion industry.[9]

After hearing the statistics, Sushila decided something must be done about the nearly ten thousand people who are trafficked from Nepal to India each year.[10] Her city is a major gateway between the two countries, and she knew she had to help. She doesn't have Facebook—she doesn't know human trafficking is a trending topic on the world stage. For someone who takes in women eating their own fecal matter, who washes their hair and trims their toenails, taking on underground crime groups and doing her part to end slavery seemed like a logical next step.

"What to do?" she says. She shrugs. "I set up booth. We help." Their booth sits at the border, and volunteers watch the stream of people, rescuing innocents from being sold once they reach India. I ask if I can see the booth.

She laughs. "It is hot there." For the last five years, three people have volunteered in that booth six days a week for eight hours a day. We pile into the small school van used for the private English-speaking elementary school they started (yes, they do that, too) and bump down the potholed, dusty road to the border. Along the way we pass people in rickshaws. They are crammed ten deep, and a skinny Nepali man, fueled only by lentils and rice, churns his legs, pouring sweat as he moves along at three miles per hour. One man on a bicycle passes our van. He is carrying hundreds of compacted cardboard boxes, and he looks like a flea pulling a sleigh. A tiny horse pulls a cart the size of a cargo van; its ribs and hipbones barely hold up its dull coat. The driver stands on the cart like a sultan or a proud chariot racer and whips it into a limping canter, the horse pulling against its too-loose harnesses, yanking the cart along.

It isn't long before we reach the booth, a blue five-foot by eight-foot corrugated metal box. It is on stilts to keep it out of the dust in the dry season and out of the mud in monsoon season—it is always one or the other in the lowlands of Nepal. There are cutout windows and a door propped open with boards. It looks a bit like a roadside snack bar, complete with an ordering window. I imagine the metal box functions more like an oven in the summertime. Three people are waiting to greet us—two women and one man. They are in long sleeves and long pants, and the women wear the traditional scarves around their necks.

The hut is lined in plywood to keep it cooler. Inside there are three picnic chairs, a small desk, and a fan, which works whenever the Nepali power grid is up and running. A gaggle of children stand outside and peer through every crevice at the white woman who has come to their roadside haunt. To document my interview I am holding my recorder, and when I see them, I grip it more tightly. I keep my phone tucked in my shirt. But I smile at them.

I am wary of children on this trip. In India, a

few weeks before, we took a motorized rickshaw home. Someone once said, "If God had made machines, he probably wouldn't have bothered with a rickshaw. It's a seven-horsepower glorified lawnmower."[11] And I agree. It is open air, with small metal bands wrapping around the carriage part of the vehicle, looking much like a dismembered gondola glued to a mini motorcycle. Rick and a friend of ours were on the outside, or the hospital-trip sides if we tipped over, and I was sandwiched safely in the middle. I was holding my bag, which contained my passport, credit cards, driver's license, and cash. I'd wrapped the strap twice around my arm. A little girl came up to the rickshaw and put her hand out. Rick reached into his pocket and said, "I will give her money, but she will shake her hand and ask for more." So he gave her four or five coins. Without looking at us, or at her hand, she shook the coins, asking for more. He said no and eventually she left. But we were still stuck in the dreaded Mumbai traffic at a light.

A few minutes passed, and a group of girls ran up to the rickshaw and surrounded it. They started calling our friend "Mother" and reaching in and touching us. When it became apparent we weren't going to give them money, they twisted their fingers in our friend's hair and pinched her arms hard enough to leave a bruise. Rick spoke calmly to me. "Don't let go; they're trying to distract you." I was angry, but not at them. I was angry at their owners.

These children's eyes were hollow and haughty. They had no fear of us or of the police. The street children in India are infamous—I'd seen documentaries about them. My friend expected sad, contrite children, but that wasn't what she found. They were brash, rough. And I knew it was because of how they'd been treated, and how they would be abused if they didn't bring home enough money from their stealing and begging. We saw many of them on the streets in India; many of them are trafficked from Nepal.

As I sit in the booth, looking at these children, I relax my grip on my things a little. They are neighborhood kids; their parents are local shop owners or buffalo herders. They are on this side of the border. I look through the window of the booth, and I can see the road clearly. Fifty yards closer to the border is a sign in front of a red brick building. The sign has big black Nepali and English letters: POLICE.

Almost 2,500 people a day take this stretch of road, and the three booth workers stare out at the traffic. The government and several other nonprofits work in tandem to scan the border, and the booths have full power to question anyone they want. The border-watchers tell me, "We run out to the street and wave. We yell at them, 'Stop! Stop!' and most of them will stop. If they do not, we call police." My American friend tells them they need a bullhorn, or at least a megaphone.

Most of the girls and boys walk alone—the

traffickers send the victims ahead while they walk behind, or they cross the border ahead and wait for them. Traffickers who are caught are potentially sentenced to twenty years in jail.[12] But it's rare they spend any time incarcerated because they threaten the victims and their families, so no one presses charges.

These girls willingly follow their traffickers. Most of their heads are filled with dreams of palaces, good jobs, abundant money. The victims are usually between twelve and eighteen years old. They are from poor families in poor villages; most are illiterate, and most are struggling to have enough to eat. They are from anywhere agents can trek and people need the money. Sometimes an agent approaches a family and offers work in India as a housemaid or as a waitress. They give the family an advance on the money they say the girl will make, and they tell them she will send funds back home from her new job.

Other times a family will knowingly sell the girl to an agent; they have too many kids and too little food. Occasionally an agent will work to develop a fake relationship with the girl, texting her, bringing her gifts, and wooing her to elope with him. A few are drugged and kidnapped. But none of the girls know the reality of what they will face once they cross the border.

Spotting a victim is easy to the trained eye. Nepalgunj is hot and dusty, and its citizens dress accordingly—loose cotton trousers and long, blousy shirts. Women and children crossing the border with a bag, who look like they've been traveling a week and are wearing woolen sweaters or peasant village clothes, are prime targets for questioning. After the workers stop the travelers, they ask them to come inside the booth for a few questions. If the potential trafficker is with them, they keep them separate for cross-questioning. They stop as many as twenty-five people a day, and they are rarely wrong.

Once a girl is in the booth, they try to develop a connection with her. They ask about her name, family, village, and friends. As the girl talks about herself, she relaxes. They ask her to explain why she is crossing the border, where she is going, and what work she will do when she gets there. Most often they recite the familiar scenario: waitress, dancer, maid, or nanny—a beautiful life with plenty of food, and money to send home. Cautiously, with sensitivity, the workers ask if the girl is aware that people are sold for money when they cross the border, but the victims never know.

After they cross the border, the sold victims will change hands about twenty-five times before they end up with their final owners. About 80 percent of those trafficked are sold for sex work. Girls go to brothels in Mumbai, Delhi, and Kolkata. Nepali women are generally lighter skinned—a desired feature in India. In the recent past, Kamathipura, in Mumbai, was one of the top destinations for sex workers. The British Empire set up India's flesh trade, deeming the brothels "comfort stations" for their officers. They sent government workers into villages to steal and purchase attractive girls as young as twelve and bring them to work. Eventually the British Raj set up brothels filled with European women to discourage mixing races. The appalling practice continued, despite much opposition, until 1947 when British rule was renounced. But when the British left, they left a booming sex trade with no oversight.

Now gangsters and crime lords rule the streets with weapons and violence. As many as twenty thousand slaves once lived in Kamathipura.[13] This notorious red light district is now home to only fifteen hundred sex workers, as the industry has diversified into other regions of the city.

The younger the victim, the more likely she is a virgin, and some people believe having sex with a virgin will cure HIV; so virgins fetch the highest price at auction. Once they reach their destination, the women and children will typically be caged for three to five years to break their independence. Once they are introduced to prostitution, they will sleep with as many as forty men a day to earn their keep.[14] Most die in a few years from abuse, torture, or malnourishment. The ones who live longer than a few years eventually die of sexually transmitted diseases. Even if a raid of rescuers finds them, they are doomed to a life of shame; they can never return home, never marry. The most they can hope for is grinding out an existence working in a sweatshop.

The very young trafficked victims are usually destined for child labor factories, or the circus to be contortionists and acrobats.[15] Some, however, only make it over the border to a hospital. Traffickers offer money (and threats) to the trafficking victims to sell or give their organs. Once procured, the trafficker sells the organs on the black market.[16]

The workers explain the simple reasons why people are sold: sex trafficking, organ harvesting, and circus work. They leave the grisly details out— the knowledge that they are about to be sold is enough. By the end of the explanation of risks, the potential victim is shaken and crying. Once they contact the family, the workers call the church and someone drives down to the border to pick the girl up. They take her to the compound and feed her, give her counseling and prayer, and wait for her parents. When the parents arrive, they educate them on the situation, but the parents never educate the rest of the village.

Marriage and childbirth provide a poor Nepali woman's main chance of survival. If the village finds out a girl was almost trafficked or even spent a week alone with a man, they shame her and she will never find husband. So the family keeps it a secret, saying the girl went to visit a relative in a neighboring village. The shame factor keeps people from educating their neighbors about the potential dangers of leaving to work in India. Most of the families are able to conceal the secret, and they are merely glad their daughters have been safely returned.

Not every story ends with reconciliation. The booth workers once rescued a girl and reunited her with her family. She said she didn't want to go home, but she was too young to go anywhere on her own, and there were no safe houses for her. When she returned home, her brothers and father were so ashamed that they beat her to death in an honor killing.[17] This haunts Sushila and KB and the workers.

After we speak, the workers tell me they are grateful I came and honored I wanted to speak with them. The feeling is mutual. Their job is crushing, every day functioning as an ominous harbinger for these vulnerable children. It wearies the soul: knowing the statistics, watching some girls still trust their traffickers, hearing about others being beaten to death. But the workers all know Kausila. They've each brought her a plate of food or had a conversation with her. They have all seen the other side of the trafficking—when the lucky ones survive physically, but not mentally. When Kausila was trafficked, no booths were at the border. They know it is easier to get the girls before they cross, so every day they sit and watch.

I wonder, with so much on her shoulders, how Sushila stays so light, how she is always smiling, and how she laughs so freely. She's the ultimate mom to thousands of people, and each one feels like they are the only one. Her grit and grin would give anyone hope—the untouchables, the smelly, the insane, the homeless. She doesn't mind scrubbing a head full of lice, clipping fingernails caked with garbage, hugging a prostitute, chasing down a trafficker renegade-style, or bringing home people that others have used as punching bags. She is not above anything, yet she carries herself like a queen. She is undiscriminating. Everyone draws the line somewhere—she doesn't. And in a time when pop psychology is focused on maintaining healthy boundaries, Sushila's gates are wide open. She isn't afraid of having enough time, food, energy, or money. She always laughs. "Only one thing makes me not laugh, makes me frustrated," she says. Her face is structured like a war chieftain with down-turned nose, a square jaw, and high cheekbones. "Selfishness," she adds.

*"Anyone who welcomes a little child
like this on my behalf welcomes me."*
Mark 9:37 NLT

DAKT—THE BOY

Rick

The gospel sometimes divides families. Jesus pointed that out when He said, "Do you think I have come to bring peace to the earth? No, I have come to divide people against each other! From now on families will be split apart, three in favor of me, and two against—or two in favor and three against. Father will be divided against son and son against father; mother against daughter and daughter against mother" (Luke 12:51–53 NLT).

But the gospel also flows through families. Jesus and John the Baptist were second cousins. James and John were brothers, the sons of Zebedee. Martha, Mary, and Lazarus were siblings. Philip the evangelist had four daughters who prophesied. The gospel is always most effective when it issues out of relationships, and families are the foundation of all relationships.

And he will turn the hearts
of the fathers to the children,
and the hearts of the children
to their fathers.
Malachi 4:6 NKJV

The boy was twelve and in his thistledown year, belligerent, moody, puzzled. He straddled the space between women and men, reluctant to cast himself into the wild. A silky wisp lay just below the surface of his upper lip. It would soon emerge, but not without a struggle. Sproutings and hatchings are never painless.

He felt fresh in the cool dawn, and his sinewy brown legs, honed through long afternoons of football on the schoolyard pitch, churned easily under him. It was a two-week trek from the Karnali River basin up into Sinja Valley. Like the fifteen men who traveled ahead of him, he shouldered his own pack. They moved fast through an endless patchwork of monsoon-saturated rice fields and sweating villages. Water buffalo bellowed angrily in the sucking muck, dragging shouting farmers and wooden plows in their wake.

He was accustomed to the annoying drone of dusk and dawn mosquitoes and the flies that sipped at the sweat on the back of his neck. They usually left a nasty bite as they departed. Impassive, he watched a cobra glide along the top of a low, distant levee. He plucked a stinging nettle as they walked and brushed it over his cousin's earlobe. His older cousin cursed him furiously, rubbing the angry welt that flushed the side of his face. They tussled a moment, awkward under their heavy packs. Just as he was about to gain enough leverage to throw his cousin to the ground, his uncle cuffed him from behind and pushed him along the trail. They walked in pensive quiet for a while until boredom breached their anger and they chattered once again. They talked of fishing in the Hima River and of pigeon traps and of the cool, sweet apples from his father's cellar.

They ascended through the foothills. He could not yet see the intimidating, snow-cloaked peaks to the north, but he knew they were ahead. The Karnali's cloudy green changed hue as they left the muddy fields of the rice plains and entered a terraced valley. By the sixth day, the holy river was a deep emerald, pure, swift, and cold. Settlements were farther apart in the upper valley, and they were careful to plan each day's journey to reach a suitable village by nightfall.

They entered the mountains after a long climb, and the terrain abruptly morphed to thick rhododendron forests and dark cathedrals of moss and lichen-covered stone. They said little, each given over to the meditative rhythm of long days on the trail and lonely stretches where few men lived. Monkeys followed them warily in the treetops, gliding in effortless rhythm through the overhead canopy, barking their warnings to the troupe farther up the valley. The river, now a clear glacial melt, thundered beside them—a constant reminder of the danger ahead. The men did not show their fear; the boy did. He knew it showed. He did not know how to hide it.

Fear stalks thin-limbed boys. Like a tiger follows the nervous dance of a tethered village goat, it tracks them from a secret canopy. Boys test themselves against one another, launching butting, tightly wound frontal assaults, but they do not test themselves against the crouching darkness. It is not an easy journey for them—that halting space between the hearth and the quest.

The group usually stopped on the trail at midday to prepare syrupy black tea and a pot of beans. They snacked on roasted soy or peanuts as they trudged through the afternoon, and at night they devoured hearty meals of the Nepali staple, dal baht, their banana-leaf plates mounded with steaming rice and lentils and whatever vegetable was in season at that altitude. Ravenous, they ate with their hands and drank black tea as they squatted around an ageless fire.

In the villages the men talked long into the night. Sometimes the men drank hot local rum, and sometimes they shouted and startled him in his sleep. But he slept deep on those cold, clear nights. He loved the mountains. He loved the mountain people. They were his people, his mountains.

His legs ached in the nights. The daily trek to school was hardly a mile, and afternoon football matches rarely lasted more than an hour or two. This marathon overtaxed him, but there would be rewards when he reached his mountain home. Already the villagers were recognizing him as his father's legacy. Though he did not yet think of himself as their leader, they would bow to him at his arrival and stoop low to touch his feet in reverence. But even in the private quiet inside their home, his father would not touch him or embrace him.

They left the dark hardwood forests and trekked through sunny patches among looming pines, following a clear, much smaller tributary of the Karnali. It was pleasant in the upper altitudes, the leeches and the sweltering heat of the flatlands a distant memory. They followed an ancient path their ancestors had blazed along a quiet narrow valley. In the valley's upper reaches, they turned east and began the grueling climb that would take them over three high ridges, one of them well above the tree line. There were difficult climbs and no villages along that route, but the shortcut would save three days. By nightfall they had reached the cave where they would spend the night.

A thousand years of nomadic campfires blackened the cave's high ceiling. It was not a deep cave, but the floor was level, and it was a good place to stop for the night. They slipped into their camp routine, he and his cousin gathering wood for the fire while his uncle readied tea. Since they were such a big group, there would be two cooking fires, so the boys gathered a large store of dry wood. His uncle balanced a pot on three blackened stones and tossed a fistful of tea into the cold water. When the pot began to steam, he reached his meaty hand into the mouth of his pack, and from the sack near the top, he scooped a generous palm of sugar. By the time the boys had gathered half the firewood, the tea was poured.

They cradled their steaming cups as they sat together in the cave mouth and watched a pair of bright sunbirds darting through the low branches of a cedar. He tossed them a piece of his chapatti, but they ignored it. An owl hooted in the darkening forest.

The boy was tired, and though he ate his beans quickly, carefully wiping the last of the spicy remnants with his chapatti, he ate without pleasure. He was not hungry. He gathered pine straw from the forest floor and fashioned a place to lie at the back of the cave. It was damp, and he shivered in the cold. He didn't know why, but he disliked the tight, confining space. Something about the stale air made him uncomfortable. He thought to lie at the front of the cave closer to the fire, but he feared the exposure.

He awoke from a night terror in the grip of the dark. He thought at first that he had dreamed, but he heard a second shout and the clamor of men roused from their sleep, and then the sharp crack of a fist to cheekbone. In the fire's waning glow, he could see the outline of his uncle's broad back as he stood in the cave mouth and bellowed into the darkness. He heard the footfalls of men retreating along the trail below the cave. He cowered against the back wall, trembling in the cold, and the fear, and the dark. The men, now fully awake, joined his uncle in the cave entrance and shouted into the darkness. There was no reply.

The men were easy targets, standing in the cave mouth and silhouetted by the fire behind them. Within moments stones were whistling out of the dark to strike with sharp pops on the cave walls. One of the men was hit just below his collarbone, and at the sickening thud of stone to chest, the boy trembled. The men took cover behind large boulders just outside the cave opening, and they began to hurl the rough flint rock that had sloughed from the cave roof and lay littered on the floor. Shouts and curses and virile threats rolled in from the darkness. The mountain bandits who had crept into their cave as they slept would not give up easily. The boy wondered what sort of weapons they might have. He imagined them rushing the cave with their machetes; their long, curving *kukri* knives;[18] and their heavy wooden staffs. He pressed himself against the cave wall.

He felt himself slipping into a sort of wakeful paralysis. He did not have the tools for this fight against men. His father would not have fought. He was a small, wiry man, but he had an authority that few men challenged. Men who knew him were afraid of him; they did not fear his fists—they feared his secret summonings. But his father was not here, and even if he were, the men who battled from below would not have respected him. They were from another place. They served other gods.

His father was a proud man, a priest. He had never seen his father cry or bend his will to another or fret the future. He ruled his little world with the impassive sternness of a sovereign. His father was untouchable.

As a baby, the boy was often ill, and on one occasion it appeared that he would die. His father gathered his assistants and consulted the spirits. The gods said they should bury the child. The priests wrapped him in a burial cloth and took him to a remote place outside the village. They dug a shallow grave and placed him in the ground. His mother told him later that he did not like it. They threw dirt over him, but they were only pretending; they wanted the spirits to think he was dead. If he were dead, there would be no need for the sickness to remain. As the men were filling the grave, his mother reached in, unwrapped him, and quickly pulled him out of the ground. She hid him under her wrap so the spirits could not see. They covered the burial cloth with earth and returned home as quickly as they could. In just a few days, he recovered. From that day forward, the boy did not like confinement.

His father rarely touched him, especially not in the presence of others. One day when he was learning to walk, he was in his home, crawling near the fire. His mother had gone to the fields that day, leaving him with his grandmother. She was supposed to watch him but had gone outside to collect water. There was a crippled man who had come to see his father for advice, and they were sitting near the fire. The boy crawled toward the fire and his father said to the man, "Remove that stone from the fire."

"What stone?" the man said.

His father pointed to the boy and said, "That stone."

It would have been dishonorable for his father to touch him. A priest is to be worshiped. He does not serve but is served. He does not honor but is honored. Even in his family he is worshiped, his wife touching his feet every morning and the children reverently bowing before him.

The next winter he was sick again, and his father carried him to a clinic in Nagma, a day's journey down the valley. In a narrow, descending section of the trail, he spotted a group of villagers approaching from below. He did not want them to see him cradling the child, so he laid his baby on the trail and hid. A flock of sheep was moving just ahead of the group of villagers, and they jostled one another in the narrow space between the mountain and the trail edge. When the lead sheep reached the child, the flock halted, unsure of what to do. The shepherds behind them shouted and hurled stones to move the flock forward. They could not see the infant lying on the trail. As the flock pressed the lead sheep from behind, some of the more impatient animals jumped the balking leads. The flock surged forward in a dusty, frantic dance and somehow passed harmlessly over the child.

Though he did not know it, the boy was wounded. Those wounds from his father were not healed, only covered over. They rankled below the surface through a lifetime. The boy did not understand that hiding a festering wound will not heal it. Like an unlanced boil concealed beneath a bandage, it will eventually burst, but before it does, it will infect the entire body with its poison.

The boy did not understand that some fathers are kings and kings do not show their flaws or their hearts. He did not understand that kings lift their gaze above the commoners to stare into an aloof horizon and issue the dictates of capricious gods and demand the obedience of nearsighted sheep.

And as the boy lay paralyzed in the dank secret corner of that cave, and as stones hurled through the night between two gangs of angry men, he prayed to his father's gods and asked them to help him. He asked for mercy.

After a long standoff, the thieves retreated, their profane taunts echoing up from the lower trail. None of them slept any more that night, and at dawn's first blush they left, cautiously picking their way up the steep climb and over a barren pass. They left without so much as a cup of tea, and it was late that evening before they ate. They force-marched two days into one, attempting to reach by nightfall a village where some of their relatives lived. They trudged into that village hours after dark, and the boy collapsed in exhaustion near a warm, safe hearth. Tomorrow night he would see his father.

Around noon the next day, they entered his valley. The big climbs behind them, they walked easily along the crystal Hima River. The water's roar gladdened him. They crossed the river on a hundred-year-old cantilevered bridge, its thick worn timbers familiar, stalwart, and comforting. He stopped for a moment and prayed before the pair of totems that stood as sentinels at the bridgehead. His forefathers had seen him safely home, and he thanked them.

It turned out to be a good summer. The monsoon rains were never as heavy up in the dry western heights as they were in the plains. Except for the swarming flies, the weather was pleasant. The days were warm and the nights cool. He fished and played football with his friends in the school-yard near the river. Though it was a good summer, his transition from boy to man was not a smooth passage.

From the time they are toddlers, boys explore the borders of their world. They probe the safety nets of their mothers' watchful care, and they test the limits of their fathers' will. In time a boy will abandon his father's design for his life and fashion his own. A wise father will give room for his son to experiment with independence and form his own horizon. An unwise father, perhaps out of insecurity or stubbornness or selfishness, will hinder that process. A foolish father will rail against his son. Little kings are reluctant to surrender their little kingdoms.

Sometimes the business of the throne distracts a father. Sometimes those fathers wound their sons. Some sons turn into men, their wounds a rite of passage. Some sons become their fathers and pass along a prideful legacy. Some sons become someone else entirely. And some sons never recover.

His father caught him stealing rice for pocket money and beat him. The boy ran and, in the furious chase, jumped into the river that ran swift through the valley below their home. His father hurried along the bank, shouting profanities until the water took him out of earshot. The boy hid in a hollow behind a large stone until his father gave up the chase. When he returned home and found that his father had not said a word to anyone of his disappearance, the boy's loathing was complete. That was the last of his carefree summers.

Native-born Israelites and foreigners
are equal before the Lord ...
This is a permanent law for you,
to be observed
from generation to generation.
Numbers 15:15 NLT

DAKT—THE MAN

Rick

A bruised reed He will not break,
and smoking flax He will not quench;
He will bring forth justice for truth.
Isaiah 42:3 NKJV

We left Dhital Lihin in mid-July, and as I stood before my father in the predawn gloom, he blessed my journey. He gave me money and laid a white *khata*[19] scarf around my neck. I stood respectfully, the night cloaking my smoldering resentment.

I imagined him there in the dark—his lean Aryan[20] face, the high cheekbones, the bright inscrutable eyes, the brown-leathered skin. He was a dark impenetrable citadel. He had no need other than to be respected. He gave no sympathy. My left eye still smarted from the thrashing of a few days before.

I admired my noble father, but I could not love him. I was beginning to understand that he was a petty man. He lived in a medieval village with no comprehension of the world that lay below him. There was not a single machine in our valley. But for our cooking pots, everything in our home was hand-fashioned. Even our knives were smithed from old truck leaf springs packed up from the Terai[21] on donkey trains.

Our return party was a much smaller group of men, so we avoided the shortcut that led us through the bandit-controlled region. It made for a longer journey, but I was grateful I did not have to face that dangerous passage. I made some decisions on that trip down. I would buy a razor, even though I was not ready to shave. I would find a way to make some money. I would not come home again until I was a man.

In the past I had dreaded the end of monsoon summer, but something changed in me that year. I was too young to stand up to my father, but I was old enough to put a plan in motion that would play out in my angst. Though grueling classes and indifferent lecturers awaited me in the sweltering lowland, for the first time I looked forward to returning.

I still despised my Sanskrit[22] lessons. I was the only student in the school studying the ancient Hindu texts. None of my forefathers could read them. I would be the first in our two-hundred-year lineage. *If I ever come back here,* I thought, *I will come back with knowledge my father does not have.* But I eventually dropped the Sanskrit anyway, preferring mathematics.

I lived with my uncle in Nepalgunj, a chaotic, dusty market town near the India border. After completing high school, I enrolled in a university on the India side. I would ride my bicycle to class from my uncle's home, and every day I passed a small building on the roadside, Sophia English Institute. I was struggling with my English so decided to take night classes to improve.

I enjoyed the classes, but I was an agitator in those days, always looking for a fight. I gave the tutor four months' advance payment for a six-month course, but after a few months, I was not happy with my progress and asked him for my money back. I was surprised that he returned my tuition without an argument. I thought he was weak. As I was leaving, he gave me a Christian booklet. I spent his money partying with my friends and threw the tract away.

Kali Basel, the school tutor, was a kind man. He was named after a Hindu goddess, the destroyer, but his gentle nature belied his namesake. He had written "Love your neighbor as yourself" on the side of his blackboard. I was a young hothead and this meek man did not impress me, but neither could I forget him. After a month I returned and told him I would like to sit in on his class but could not pay. He surprised me again, saying, "OK."

"Love your neighbor as yourself" troubled me. My uncle was a wealthy man and politically connected. He constantly fought with his neighbor in a property dispute. Both men had threatened one another. I lived in fear. My uncle organized his four sons and me to defend against a gang attack. His home was a terrifying place. I did not think it was possible to love your neighbor.

Kali gave me a second little booklet and said, "Bring this back when you finish it and I'll give you another one."

I'd collect a new booklet every visit. It was a Bible correspondence course, and though much of the material was difficult to understand, it touched me. In a short time, I decided to become a Christian. I dropped the language class but started attending Kali Basel's little church.

Those were pleasant days. The Christian people were not what I expected. As a Brahmin,[23] I had an arrogance that I was not even aware of until many years later. Pastor KB, as we called him, patiently tolerated my bad behavior and taught me the Christian way of life. Their way was better. They were kindhearted, respectful people, and they treated one another with a gentle grace that I had never seen before. I threw myself into my newfound faith, and in a short time, I was put in charge of tract distribution. I loved what I was doing.

It wasn't long before my uncle discovered my conversion. I was living such an inspired life that I often prayed in my dreams. We lived in a small house, and we boys all slept in the same room. They heard me speaking Jesus' name as I slept.

My uncle threatened me and sent word to my father that I was now a Christian. Of course, this made my father very angry, but there was no communication between us. A few weeks later, my uncle roused me out of bed and brought me into the main room of the house. He had gathered a group of his friends, and they had been drinking.

"Do you love us, or do you love this Jesus?" they demanded.

"I love you, and I love Jesus," I said. I was frightened. They were shouting at me, threatening to beat me, and they were angry. I had been awakened from a deep sleep, so it took me a few moments to collect my thoughts.

"You must love one or the other," my uncle said. "You cannot love both."

"I love Jesus first, and I love you second."

That did not satisfy them. They grew furious and all began to beat me, their blows unpredictable, coming from every direction. There were too many of them for me to fight. I tried to protect myself as my body absorbed their drunken strikes. They pushed me out of the house and into the yard and told me never to come back. I was banished.

It was pouring rain that night, and I stumbled down the lane that led from my house. Lightning struck a tree just as I turned onto the main road, and it fell across the road in front of me. It seemed as if the entire world had turned against me. With hatred thick around me and fear lodged in my throat, I wept bitterly. The blinding hurt, and rage, and the deep abandoned feeling were difficult to understand. I had never felt so alone. I stumbled down the empty main road, heaving in grief, my tears mingling with the cold monsoon rain.

I found my way to the church and knocked. Pastor KB and his family lived in a little room that was partitioned off within the church building. It was a pitiful little place with a leaky roof, but it was pleasant compared to outside. It was the only place I knew to go.

Pastor KB was in Kathmandu. His wife, Sushila, gave me hot tea and prayed with me, but I could not spend the night. When the rain slackened, I walked the three miles to my university, where I slept in the boys' dorm with my friends. Three days later they found out I was a Christian, and they got angry too. I moved in with Pastor KB and his family.

That was a dangerous time for all of us. My uncle and my cousins would often call KB and threaten him, saying they were going to kill him. Over the next few months, everyone in my family disowned me. My father pretended as if I had never lived. Except for one brief visit when he met Pastor KB, I did not hear from my father for seven years.

A father's love is a difficult thing to understand. I think my father must have once loved me, but I suppose I embarrassed him. His pride would not allow tender affection. I don't know why fathers are that way. I decided I would not command my children or intimidate them or strike them in anger. I would never be like him, I thought, but the more I tried to be unlike him, the more I was like him. I would hear his voice in my voice, and hear his words in my head, and feel his anger in my heart.

I thought forgiveness would be easy. I knew it was the right thing to do—*love your neighbor as yourself, love your enemies, honor your father and your mother.* I made that decision at the front of the church, kneeling before the congregation and pouring genuine tears onto the floor. I prayed sincerely; I thought I forgave completely. I tried to believe with all my heart, but I hurt deeply. When I met my uncle by chance on the street, I avoided him, shaking in anger. Forgiveness, it turned out, was not such an easy thing.

I wish I could say that I loved my enemies during that brokenhearted season, but I cannot. I would tremble in rage if I happened to see my uncle or any of my relatives. I was angry with my father. Pastor KB and Sushila helped me find a gentler way, but it took years to change my behavior. The journey from religion to grace was difficult.

During my time there, I fell in love with a young girl named Sobha. I told no one. KB approached me one day and said, "What do you think about Sobha?"

"Is that possible?" I asked. I knew that if Pastor KB was approaching me about her, he and Sushila must have seen some interest on her part. Nothing could have made me happier.

When I printed our wedding invitations, I hand delivered one to my uncle. His eyes filled with tears when I gave him the card, and he said, "I did wrong to you. I am sorry."

His remorse helped me heal from the pervasive sadness that gripped me, but my father lingered, distant and disapproving, in his mountain stronghold. He did not attend our wedding.

My father fell ill—asthma. Jumla's thin air taxed him, and his family brought him down to the hospital in Nepalgunj. I heard he was sick and felt it was an opportunity to demonstrate God's power to my father. I would pray for him and the Lord would heal him, and he would witness my God's authority. I walked to the hospital in great anticipation.

His emaciated form shocked me. He lay unconscious on a narrow bed, a frail medieval man under the efficient care of a twenty-first-century respirator. As the hushed piston-like machine wheezed, I laid my hand on my father to pray, but I could not. I wept like a child.

I entered that room thinking I would be bold and faith-filled and courageous. I thought I would demonstrate the power of God. I thought there would be a miracle and that my father would see his error and repent and ask for my forgiveness. I thought I would lead him into my new religion and convert him to my better way of life. But when I touched him, a flood of brokenness and grief eclipsed me. I felt sorry for him, weak and frail and needful.

After a long while, my father awakened and saw me standing beside his bed. Without a word he turned away. *Still angry*, I thought. *He is in his last moments and he cannot, will not, speak.* It was difficult to understand. My heart ached for him, and for myself, and for our broken love.

I brought my father to my home and cared for him. For three months he stayed with my wife and me and our baby in our single rented room. In time he began to smile. I was hopeful.

My father was too frail to survive the mountain winters and began to spend the winter months with us in Nepalgunj. He fell in love with his granddaughter and would carry her on his shoulders, even in public. He didn't care who saw him or what they thought. He loved without restraint. Finally, on one Christmas Day, my father gave his heart to the Lord.

I had thought he would become a Christian through some miracle. I had thought I would pray for him and he would see the power of my faith and convert. But it did not happen as I expected. I did not work a miracle, except to love him and to care for him and to forgive him. And that was miracle enough.

"Who has done such mighty deeds,
summoning each new generation
from the beginning of time?
It is I, the Lord, the First and the
Last. I alone am he."
Isaiah 41:4 NLT

DEEPNATH—THE PRIEST

Rick

And you will be my kingdom of priests, my holy nation.

Exodus 19:6 NLT

I sat with Deepnath on the steep slope above his village. A glacial stream whispered from a half mile below. Across the valley, almost eye level with us, I could make out the high grass plateau and the crumbled foundation of a thousand-year-old palace. This valley junction was an important stronghold. From our position we could see several miles up and down the Hima River and at least a mile up an adjacent gorge to the northeast. Whoever controlled this choke point controlled access to an important northern trade route and pass over the Himalayas. It was only an eight-day trek from here to Tibet.

During the Maoists' rebellion, this village was an important command post. Below us were the ruins of a crumbling old tunnel. The Maoists had constructed it as an escape route out of the village, laying timbers across the narrow ravine and covering them with stony earth. Even up close it was barely discernible. If you didn't know it was there, you would not likely notice it. Whenever the rebels spotted the Nepali army advancing up the valley, they would scramble through the tunnel to escape into the mountains. Deepnath and I had ascended the hill through that tunnel, up through a steep, narrow channel to the place we now sat.

On one of my earlier visits, when the Maoists were still active, he had shown me a weapons cache in his rock-hewn water-buffalo stall, a shallow cave below his home. The rebels had stored grenade launchers, AKs, and ammunition there. "If you touch it," they had told him, "we will kill you."

"If the Nepali army finds it, they will kill me," he had said. Like many folk in the developing world, he was vulnerable, caught between two warring ideologies. It didn't matter that he was not political.

We sat cross-legged in the grass, resting below a decrepit two-hundred-year-old structure. He called it a temple, but really it was a shrine, maybe twenty square feet. Prayer flags fluttered in the wind above it, and within there were several scowling, dark stone idols. Ancient Sanskrit had been carved into its weathered stones.

I asked him to tell me his story. He looked back at the old shrine and shrugged. With a stoic sigh, he turned back around to gaze thoughtfully down the valley. After a long while he spoke.

My ancestors came here about two thousand years ago from Āryāvarta, "the abode of the Aryans." It's in what is now called Iran. No Mongolian people were living in this valley then. An ancient king built his palace here, and the ruins across the valley are all that remain. He had another palace in Hatsinja, on the way to Mugu from Rara. You went through there when you hiked to Mugu with the brothers. His kingdom stretched from Pokhara to western Nepal and from the Terai to the Tibet border. They say that he buried treasure somewhere near here, but no one has found it.

The king's treasure was part of a banking system he used to administer the trans-Asia trade passing through this region. That word is called *dhito*, meaning "bank" in Nepali. My family name, Dhital, is derived from that word. My forefathers managed an ancient banking system.

After many generations, King Nagraj from central Nepal conquered this area. He eventually moved his palace to Kathmandu and from there united all of Nepal. Throughout these kings' reigns, the Jumla people worshiped the goddess Sundari, the "Beautiful Goddess."[24] In late October they would sacrifice male water buffalos to her. Though that kingdom ceased long ago, we continued to practice the sacrificial buffalo ritual.[25] Our tradition was to drive the animals down to a place on the riverbank where we would sacrifice them. The route took the animals through our rice fields right at harvest time. The procession destroyed some of the rice.

My forefather, four generations back, introduced a new goddess to our valley and started a new form of worship that did not include this ritual sacrifice. Most of the people accepted it, but there were some who fought the new ideas. The case went to the Nepali court, and my forefather won the decision. The judgment was written on a twenty-four-foot-long scroll. We still have one copy of that two-hundred-year-old document. I gave the other copy to the Department of Archaeology. With that judgment my forefather inaugurated a new form of worship and built this temple. His priesthood has been passed from father to son since that time, and I had hoped that my son Dakt would take over my priesthood.

We follow tradition here. Our oldest scriptures were written thirty-five hundred years ago. We've been a civilization on this continent for over five thousand years. We could not have this long history without a strong loyalty to our way of life. Though foreigners have conquered us, we have always prevailed. It is important to us that our sons and daughters follow our ways. I did everything in my power to teach those ways to my children.

Once a year the people would carry me up to this site on their shoulders. They would bathe me in milk and place me in the temple. They would worship me as a god, a holy man. Then I would sit naked here in the temple, and the gods would enter me. I would tremble, and afterwards I would prophesy to them and give them messages from the gods. They would do anything I told them to do. I tried to lead them as best I could.

Most of my ministry to the people did not take place here, but down in the village. There is an old house there that my ancestor built when he built this temple. The people would come to me for horoscope readings and for blessings. I would sit on a throne there, and we would worship with singing and drums and music. The house had a stone floor, and under my seat was a hollow space that led to a channel in the bedrock. Sometimes when I sat there, a snake would come up through that channel and coil in the hollow space beneath me. I don't know where he came from; he would just appear. The snake was real, but not always the same color, and sometimes it was golden. It had a mane on its head like a horse's mane. I was afraid of the snake, but I liked when it came. It made me feel powerful. When the people worshiped the snake, they also worshiped me.

As a priest, I would rise early, wash myself, and ring the temple bell. The villagers would come to worship the idols with offerings: flowers, fruits, and incense. They would often lay flowers on my legs as I sat before them, and I would bless them. They were afraid of me, afraid that I would curse them, but I never saw any reason to curse anyone.

The Tibetans who live north of us follow different gods. In our region, everyone believes in the Tibetan gods, but we believe our gods rank higher. Sometimes I would travel north to worship in the Tibetan temples, and every year they would journey down to my village to pour milk on my head and honor me.

My first wife was much younger than me. She did not please me, so I took a second wife, an older woman. One day my second wife took one of my first wife's favorite dresses and cut it into little pieces. My first wife brought the cloth to me and said, "Who cut my dress?"

"Obviously, a rat did not do this," I said. "You know who did it. Take the cloth to the temple."

She made a sacrifice in the temple and told everything to a priest, who cursed my second wife. In just a few days, my second wife went insane and died not long after. From that time on, my family members began to die until my first wife and I were the only ones remaining. My home became like a haunted house, and unexplainable things began happening. Sometimes my bed would shake, sometimes the doors would mysteriously open or close, and sometimes I would awake to find mud splattered on my family's old photos.

My oldest son had moved to Nepalgunj, down in the plains, and I heard he had become a Christian.

I was not happy about that, and I stopped communicating with him. I could not understand why he had chosen to follow the foreigners' god.

A few years later, I traveled through Nepalgunj on my way to India, and my son asked me to visit him. He was staying with a Christian pastor, KB Basel, and we met in his home. They prepared a big meal for me, and they treated me well. He started telling me about the gospel, but I wouldn't listen. I argued with him. "I'm a Hindu priest," I said. "Our gods are powerful. I know their power. They are real."

My son said, "Father, you are having so much trouble. You can't sleep at night. Spirits are coming to your house. One of your wives died. You are sick. There is so much trouble in your life. If you will accept Jesus, all these troubles will go away."

They gave me a little book, *The Reality of Life*, and I took it with me to India. I read it during my three months there, but I did not stop in Nepalgunj on my way back home. When I reached home, I found that my wife was sick. It seemed as if she might die. She wanted to go to Nepalgunj to see if the Christians could heal her. We argued about it. I told her she should stay here with her people. If she died, she would die here where she belonged, not among strangers who did not follow our ways.

She went anyway, and in a few months, she was healed. She did not want to come home, which made me angry. After about a year, she sent a message that I should come to Nepalgunj. I was sick, too, by then and had lost weight. We both had breathing problems, which are common in our area. The medical people tell us it is because we cook over wood fires and do not vent our homes. It is true that our homes are often smoke-filled, but we have lived this way for centuries. There are many old people in our villages.

I did not go to Nepalgunj when she invited me, but after some months I became so sick that my relatives thought I would die. They took me down to the plains, which in those days was a long journey. They had to carry me for over a week on a litter. Along the way I passed in and out of consciousness, and in Nepalgunj they put me on a ventilator.

I awoke one afternoon in the hospital. I was weak and my throat was parched. I turned on the bed to see my oldest son sitting in a chair beside me, weeping. We looked into each other's eyes and he smiled. He seemed nervous. I watched him for a moment and then turned my back to him.

A father spends his life preparing a way for his son. A good father leaves his son an inheritance and a legacy. I had given him everything. I had been strong for him. I had disciplined him and shown him how a man should live. I had given him an education better than my own. I had taught him how to lead our people, how to read the stars, how to administer herbal medicines, and he had shamed me.

I could not understand why he was weeping. Men do not weep. He had grown weak living here in the plains. This foreign god had made him into something else. *He has forgotten everything I taught him*, I thought. *He is not who I made him to be.*

I decided in that moment that I would never accept his wife or visit his children or approve of his life here. I did not care that my wife was healed. I would rather die than be humiliated before my people. I felt nothing for him. *He is no longer my son*, I thought.

The patient next to me in the men's ward was dying. He lay on his back barely a half-meter away, his hideous mouth gaping open. I could smell his cancerous stench. I counted his laboring breaths, and I swore to myself that I would not die in this hellhole. *I have no son and I have no wife*, I thought. *When I am better, I will leave them all here. I will die in my mountains, among my people. I will not die among these strangers.*

Deepnath paused, reflecting on what he had said. I didn't comment, but I marveled at how stubborn folk can be in their traditions. The sun had dropped behind the ridge across the valley at about four in the afternoon, and though there was still good light, it had started to get cold. In the big mountains, the ridges block the early-morning and late-evening sun, making the days much shorter. In some of the deeper, narrower valleys, there are hardly more than four hours of direct sunlight. We were up around nine thousand feet. In early winter the temperature drops quickly at that altitude. We still had a few hours of indirect daylight, but we were without our jackets and Deepnath was thin. I feared he might chill.

"Let's go down," I said. "We can finish the story later."

We sat around a fire that night in his hovel of a home. The fire pit was nothing more than a hollowed-out place in the hard-packed dirt floor, and smoke-blackened, hand-hewn timbers buttressed the roof above us. After a long cold night, we would spend our morning on that flat rooftop, warming in the crisp sun. The roof was a primitive structure: straw over timbers, a layer of compressed earth, a layer of slate, and a final layer of sifted dirt mixed with dung. It leaked when the rains were heavy, but it seldom rains in the dry northwest.

A young blind teenager prepared our meal. He was from a nearby hostel that I was yet to visit. He fussed about the fire in complete darkness, feeling his way with his hands. I turned on my flashlight and then felt foolish when Deepnath joked that the boy didn't need any light. I knew very little about him, but I would get to know him later. In some ways he changed my life. I will never forget him. I was anxious about his cooking and wondered what he was tossing into the pot. I should not have fretted; the meal was delicious.

We finished our meal and went to bed early. It was cold, well below freezing, and in the unheated house, my breath was a vapor. I ignored the rat rummaging in the corner and snuggled into a down sleeping bag for the night.

..."I lavish unfailing love
for a thousand generations
on those who love me
and obey my commands."
Exodus 20:6 NLT

DEEPNATH—THE FATHER

Rick

And a voice from heaven said,
"This is my dearly loved Son,
who brings me great joy."
Matthew 3:17 NLT

Those early visits were the beginning of a curious relationship. Deepnath and I are the same age, and both of us tend to old-man sentimentalities. My first trips to his place were grueling: a harrowing mountain flight followed by an eleven-hour trek over several high-altitude ridges. I once walked up from where the north road ended. It took three days. I usually got to his home well after midnight. These days there is a road, and the journey is easier when there is a bus running; but with landslides and political conflicts, it's still uncertain.

A few days later, Deepnath and I would embrace one another and weep. He always does that to me. He will say, "I don't know if I will be here next time you come."

And I will say, "I'll see you again next year, my friend." And we will weep again, and he will lay a garland around my neck. And later, when I have hiked a few hours, I will throw the garland into the Hima River. That river joins the Karnali, which joins the Ganges, the Hindu holy river that flows through India to Calcutta.

A year after that visit, I received a handwritten letter from him—the meticulous Hindi script arranged in perfect lines. It was written on an aerogram. He had gotten sick again.

Beloved of the Lord and my beloved,

Greetings from Huma Church. I came from Jumla to Nepalgunj in February. I was sick and about to die. Pastor KB, Sushila, my son, and Mohan helped me to go to the hospital, and by God's grace I am alive today. I thought of you while I was dying. God gave me victory over death.

When you left from my house to walk to Rara, I cried because I thought I might never see you again. I am praying I will see you again. I am praying for you. God showed His love to me, and more than this, God loves you also. I am praying for your welfare and that you may have a long life. Thank you for coming to the very remote places of the world.

The blind children[26] are blessed through your ministry. You are trying to transform this place. People are sleeping here. We are thankful to God for your heart. I am praying always with tears. If I die, I request that you keep doing this work. The church is growing here.

I am not educated, and I am not a gifted man. Thank you for teaching us good things. I am so thankful for you. I will never forget your help and your kindness to the people here. Keep praying for me. I am not strong. I am very far from you as I write, but I am not far from you.

Your beloved,

Deepnath

My dear Nepali friend thinks more like a grandfather these days. He weeps often, he has regrets, and he shows great joy when he holds his grandchildren. We organize annual meetings in Nepalgunj where we gather about ten thousand church members for three days. I can always spot him in the crowd when I am speaking. He sits cross-legged on the ground with a serene smile, taking careful notes. He is not the angry man he once was. He seems to have found that deep, restful peace that so few find. He is an admirable father.

Most men are love-starved for their fathers. They spend their lives searching for that love, and their frustrations often surface in their temper, their impatience, their damaged relationships. Deepnath never knew that sort of love, and for many years he vented his frustrations on his hapless firstborn. He feels some shame over that now, but he should not be ashamed. He just didn't know. His son is a good man.

We hiked the next day to a nearby village where Deepnath had started a little house church. It was about a four-hour journey, but we were not due till afternoon. We had planned to spend the night in the village, so we traveled slowly, pausing once for a bowl of beans, and often to chat. It was a pleasant journey along a clear, swift-running river. As we sat under the shade of a sprawling oak, he told me the rest of his story.

I was angry when I did not recover in the hospital. My son came every day to visit me, and he stayed a few nights, sleeping on the floor. Sometimes he would lay his hand on my shoulder and pray for me. I pretended to sleep.

After a few days, the doctor took me off the ventilator. They made me breathe from a machine that had medicine in it. The medicine would come out of the machine like smoke. It was a vapor, like the fog of a hot spring, and it helped my breathing. In a week I left the hospital and went to my son's house in Nepalgunj. It was a small rented house, only one room. My wife and I stayed there with my son Dakt, his wife, and their baby.

Though I hardly spoke to him, my son was caring. His wife was a good woman, and she never complained about me. I recovered and thought about returning to my home in the mountains, but I was beginning to enjoy the church people. They were kind to me.

One evening while we drank tea together, my son told me he forgave me. That angered me. What had I done that required his forgiveness? He was the one who had wronged me. He should have asked me to forgive him. But the more I lived among the Christians, the more I realized that I had wronged him in many ways. I began to feel sorry for some of the things I had said to him, and I regretted the times when I had hit him.

That winter, on Christmas Day, I attended a meeting with the Christians. There were many of them, and they had prepared a meal with roasted meat. Someone gave me a heaping plate of *biryani*[27] with a choice piece of lamb hidden in the rice. The man who had given me the biryani was a Brahmin, like me, but he served me humbly. The Christians did not follow caste. They treated everyone equally. They were humble, forgiving of one another, and generous.

As I sat among them, I felt ashamed. I realized I was not a good man. I had abused many people, my son most of all. I asked God to forgive me, and later I asked my son to forgive me. I became a Christian that day.

After winter passed I returned to my village, but I was ignorant. I gathered all the villagers together and commanded them to become Christians. They grew angry and nearly beat me. I had so many things to learn.

I wondered how I could survive in that place. There are thousands of villages where I live and many people, but my wife and I were the only Christians. I found a place in the Bible that says, "Where two or three gather in my name, there am I with them."[28] I told my wife that two were enough.

I began spending my winters with my son, where I learned the Christian ways. I spent the planting and harvest seasons in the mountains. In time I became a pastor and started a little church in my home, but I was still weak in my body and often sick.

The haunting spirits left my house. Slowly my life improved, but I wondered about my future. Though I was now a Christian, I still clung to some of my old religious beliefs. In our culture, when a person dies, he is cremated. His ashes are filtered, then poured into a large bowl and covered with a basket. In the morning the priest will visit and lift the basket cover. In the ashes there will be a sign indicating what that person will become in the next life. I wondered who would do these things for us. What would happen when we died?

It was during this time that my wife passed away. The winters are very difficult where we live. Though my son and Pastor KB felt she should stay in Nepal-gunj during the winter, she and I thought that she was strong enough. We decided we would spend that winter in the mountains. We were wrong. I regret that decision, and at first I was ashamed that I had not insisted that we stay in the south during the cold months. But we all make mistakes in life. We cannot return to those mistakes and correct them. We must live with their consequences.

I found grace to live through that difficult time. I wrote my wife's life story, and I read it at her funeral. It was a powerful and emotional experience for me. Our people do not often express their love publicly, and it surprised them that I spoke so openly about her. They all knew me as their village priest. They knew of my pride and my harsh leadership. To see my contrition and my humility confused them at first.

I told them of my regrets, of the changes that had come so late in my life, of how I found my wife's forgiveness when I apologized to her for my sins, and of how I found God's grace. Many people were weeping at her funeral, and many of them became Christians afterwards.

I grew ill two winters after my wife died. My sister was staying with me at that time, helping to care for me. I told her that I thought I would die. I was tired, and I longed to join my wife. I missed her. That night I must have died. At the least, I went into a sort of coma. It is difficult to say what happened. My description is not very adequate.

I found myself in a place filled with bright light

and music. I have never heard music like that. In our villages we play local made stringed instruments and double reed horns. We play drums fashioned from animal hides. But this music was different. There were instruments I had never heard, very high voices, and very deep voices. It was something like the sound of a river mingled with the wind, but all the tones harmonized and moved together. I was only there a short while.

Someone came from behind and pushed me from that place. I fell down toward a large burning field, and as I approached the field, I swooped up like an eagle does when he is about to catch a hare. I soared over that field, and it seemed endless. At first I could not see them, but when I looked more closely, I realized there were multitudes of people standing in the field. They were standing in fields of fire, and they were looking up at me as if they were expecting me to do something for them. It was very disturbing.

Suddenly I found myself walking near my house. I entered my home, and I saw my body lying on the bed. My sister was kneeling beside it, saying, "My brother has left me here alone."

I walked over to my body, and I touched my mouth. My mouth opened when I touched it, and somehow I went into my body. I opened my eyes and saw my sister and all my people standing around my bed. They said, "How is it that you are breathing? You have been dead for twenty-five minutes!"

Now, I think about dying every day. I speak of it often. It is not a bad thing. It is a wonderful place. I am eager to go there, but I understand that a great work remains for me. There are many people who stand in flaming fields waiting to hear my words.

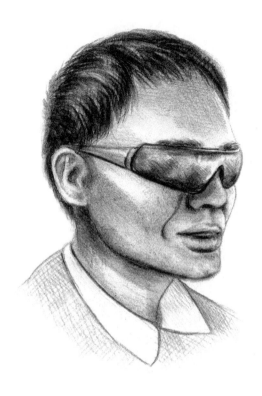

I will bring honor to your name
in every generation.
Therefore, the nations will praise you
forever and ever.
Psalms 45:17 NLT

GANESH

Bev

Nepal is an amazing ethnic quilt of a place. There are well over one hundred tribal groups and castes. This is Buddha's birthplace. The Hinduism practiced here may be the most accurate living example of Mesopotamian Babylon. The Tibetan-influenced mountain shamans follow carefully preserved prehistoric rites little changed for five thousand years. And yet Nepal, in the dawn of the twenty-first century, is one of the fastest-growing Christian communities in the world. Their worship is raw and emotional and enthusiastic.

Some of my most memorable times of worship have been in the pristine, darkened theaters of large Western congregations where the musicians are artists and the sound and light flawless. But I often find, when I close my eyes in those sanctuaries, that my heart is filled with memories of simple moments with unsophisticated tribal folk in forgotten, unmapped villages.

At first appearance, Ganesh bears no resemblance to the Hindu god for whom he is named, who is often shown as a giant blue elephant and known as the remover of obstacles. His torso is small, giving his upper body the semblance of a birdcage from which the bird grew but the cage did not, and now his lanky arms and legs sprawl out from between the bars of his ribs. He is slight and smiling, his triangle beak of a nose peeking out from under dollar-store plastic tourist glasses. They hide his blind eyes.

"So, Ganesh. Ganesh what? What is your last name?" I ask, fingers on my keyboard, ready to type.

After a few pronunciations and disagreements on letter sounds, I land on "Devkorta."

"Yes," Ganesh agrees. "Devkorta." He explains the name origin. Two brothers lived in a mountain region long ago. The older brother decided he was priestly—not working, only writing and praying to his idol. The younger brother worked in farming. One day the priestly brother went to worship his idol, but he could not find it. The working brother admitted he had destroyed the idol. He was tired of the priestly brother's laziness.

"Name is *Dev*, meaning 'god.' *Korta* meaning 'beater.' God killer. Working brother killed praying brother's god." Ganesh chuckles and leans forward in his seat. I've already learned so much of his family and cultural history, just from his last name, but that's how Nepal is—tradition is thick, sometimes even catching in the gears of progress and change, slowing them down.

Ganesh's palms are propped on his hot-pink guide stick, and I wonder if he knows it is hot-pink, or if he knows what that color looks like, or if—in Nepal, a country teeming with bold colors—hot-pink is even considered a feminine color. And if it were considered a feminine color, I wonder if he would be offended. I decide he would not. It only takes a minute to see he is singularly sweet, the way honey is good on its own. He is happy.

We are quiet at first, and I watch a lazy mosquito take its time whirring around Ganesh's head, not being seen, not being shooed away. It chooses an ear, and Ganesh smiles and reaches to swat it. In the serenity of the moment I take a deep breath and I smell the livestock next door.

Nepal is a middling nation, landlocked by China and India like a young boy stuck between two older bullies, jostled on its bumpy ride through history. It's long been a haven to travelers—but those travelers come for the mountains, not the lowlands, which is where we are. Nepalgunj is all humidity and animals and ticks. Water buffalo trudge through rice fields, breaking fat fronds, pressing them into the muck. Gaze into any puddle left from monsoon season, and watch the jerk and twitch of mosquito larvae, biding their time to vampire. It is human against beast and dust, a daily ruling clock of cooking, laundry, working in the dirt, and working to remove the dirt. As the sun sets and the oppressive heat gives its final shove before bowing to night, Nepali women squat barefooted on their porches and slosh water over the stoops, swishing with their long bristled brooms. They tame the grime. I can hear them swishing now.

But we are in a compound delineated by a thick concrete wall, a realm of peace, "a rich jewel in an Ethiop's ear," to quote Shakespeare. There are a school, a few large houses, a few church buildings, and a pristine, empty grass field within the walls. This field is an oddity in a land where poor farmers have long forced every inch of turf into an agricultural stream—even if only a dribble—of income. Just outside the compound, I hear tiny, gaunt horses pulling probably fifteen people on an old wooden jaunting car.[29] On the compound where I am, there is a pair of pearl-colored, air-conditioned SUVs.

I sit with Ganesh on a clean, tiled porch under a churning fan at a large, beautiful glass-topped table, anachronistic if it were outside the compound. The contrast, even five feet away from where I sit, is startling. There is a water pump off the porch, and young girls come to get buckets of water for laundry and cooking. They grin at us and gather curious bits of conversation to take to their friends; within the compound one of the most exciting things happening today is the Americans' conversation with Ganesh. A woman brings green tea for us, and we leave it covered to keep the flies, crickets, no-see-ums, mosquitos, gnats, and butterflies out.

I already know part of Ganesh's story. I'd done as much research as I could before we met—that word-of-mouth Nepali way, the old way, the story-telling way. We get quiet, and I remember watching him sing at a conference a few days before. His voice was taut, evenly pitched, with no showboat vocal runs like we have in America. His dissonant vibrato wavered, characteristic of Nepali vocalist style. That day he had trouble with microphone distance, and in the middle of the song, a pastor walked up behind him and put a hand on his shoulder and urged him closer to the mic. Ganesh didn't startle, and I realized it was normal for him to feel touch with no warning, even in the middle of giving a performance in front of ten thousand people.

He was born in Humla, a small mountain town

in the foothills of the Himalayas. He went to a school for the blind in another village about a week's journey away from the one where he was born. He sings. He likes computers. That is all I know.

"You like computers?" I'm grasping at common ground.

"I am learning. Microsoft Office. I want an Apple company's computer," he says.

"You went to a school for the blind?"

"Yes. When I was thirteen."

"What was life like before the school?" I watch his features change perceptibly, and I almost regret asking. I want to develop a connection before we start wading through the tough stuff.

"It was painful. Miserable. Difficult to describe. It was like wilderness. No meaning to life."

I decide to change course; that door doesn't feel open yet. I bring it back to a pleasant topic—the school seems to be the dividing line for him between darkness and light. "How did you find the school?"

The corner of his mouth quirks up, and humor plays on his face. "I was wedding singer. People tell me I have no life, so I work weddings so I can party and drink and smoke to die." Ganesh knew no one would give him medical treatment if he became sick, and he knew the alcohol in Nepal is poor quality, cut with deadly chemicals. He'd heard of many beggars in his community who drank their lives into a coma and slipped into death, and he'd planned that life for himself. "But a man came to Humla to visit. He saw me, young boy, with party, tobacco, and alcohol."

The man offered Ganesh a rare piece of musical equipment, a drum, which could get him more wedding gigs. The man had two stipulations before he would give him a drum: no alcohol, no tobacco. Over the next few months, he quit both, and he proved it to the man the next time he visited. But the man pulled a bait-and-switch. "I can give you the drum you want. Or . . . I can help find you a school."

"You chose school," I prompted.

"I thought, if man bring me drum, rat may eat drum. Drum may break, get old. School will remain. Cannot take learning away," he said.

I asked about his parents' religious affiliation. It was a given, being from the villages and even being from Nepal, a country known as one of the last true Hindu kingdoms.

"Yes. Hindu." He was not born blind; he contracted a virus, which blinded him at ten months old. "Parents seek witch doctor, but no one can fix me."

I asked where Hindus believe blindness comes from.

"Many beliefs. Some think in my past life I caused mischief. Some think my parents did some mischief. Others think because of stars, astrology, I am supposed to be handicapped. They think when my light went out, it was justice. Darkness is my punishment."

"As a baby," I say. "Punishment for someone else's sin?" And he nods.

"Yes. I was cursed. They want me to go to school, be gone." So he left.

He and his older brother made the journey from Humla to Jumla together, a difficult route of mountain passes and forests. He stumbled barefooted over the rocky terrain, breaking toes and twisting his ankles. Eventually his toenails blackened and dislodged from their beds, and his brother decided to carry him on his shoulders. They had no water to cook their food, and they slept unprotected in the forest. It took them six days to reach Jumla, and his new school.

"I will never forget my first day of school. I thought now my life is changing. Great hope has come. No boundary of happiness, so happy I was. I felt like my eyes are open now. My life is now bright, I thought." That night he went home to the hostel where he lived. He never slept. He picked up his Braille books, and even though he couldn't read, he brushed his fingers over the bumps, crying over the pages, worrying he would ruin them with his tears. "I will never forget that day," he says again. "Never."

"My parents did not miss me when I moved. I was like dead man."

Twenty days after he started school, winter holiday began. He could not go home because it was too long of a trip for his family to transport him to and from Jumla. The man who'd offered him a drum, and then school, lived two hours from the town, so he invited Ganesh to stay with him that first winter. The man had a small two-month-old daughter, and Ganesh babysat during the holiday.

After a few years of his parents journeying across mountains and jungles, for a total of twelve travel days each time to and from school, they decided the trip wasn't worth it anymore. "'What are you going to do anyway after you are done?' they asked me. There was no future, they thought." Ganesh leans back in his chair and lays his cane on the ground.

"I had trunk there. It is the only reason I could keep going back every semester." It was a small metal box containing his most precious items—a few dolls and a spoon he'd found. He often wondered if he died, who would take care of his trunk. Every break, he'd leave his box at school on purpose, and every time his parents refused to take him back to school, he told them he'd at least have to retrieve his trunk. They were upset, but they'd take him back, and Ganesh would stay to finish the semester. It worked every time, for all eight years of his schooling, until he completed his education.

"I never fail class. Always, I pass," he says. "I'd planned. I was happy in school, but I would graduate in two years. I thought I would find city, become monk, and beg." Ganesh had found a short reprieve from his previous death wish. He'd gained friends and a high school education, but he saw no future beyond that. The begging monk's life was a hard one, and they usually lived no more than two years before getting ill, not receiving treatment, and dying. "At least I was eighteen. I could have big monk beard before I died," he says, and we laugh.

I ask him about his faith. Sitting on a Christian compound, he was a long way from Jumla and his parents' beliefs.

"At first, I leave faith. If God is real, why am I this way? That is how I thought. But a man came to me." Deepnath had visited the school for the blind to spend time with Ganesh's Christian friend and fellow student, Datta. Deepnath spoke to Ganesh about Jesus, but Ganesh refused to believe.

Eight months after he met Deepnath, Datta and Ganesh traveled to the main town by bus. He stuffed a book bag with all of the money he had, six thousand Nepali rupees, so he could purchase supplies while he was in town. He lost his bag and all of his new, valuable supplies. Datta and Ganesh searched the bus and couldn't find the bag, so they went to the police. The police couldn't locate it either, and considering the circumstances, there was no hope.

"I told my friend, if your god is real, tell him to find my bag," he says. "My friend say all right, he would pray." And three days later, Ganesh's bag appeared at the police station, containing almost everything he'd left in it. It was a simple deal he'd made—his soul for six thousand rupees and a few supplies. "But," he says, "the thief took one thing from me. One pair of brand-new underwear. I went to church that day and became Christian."

"Despite the underwear thief?" I ask.

"Yes! No matter that I lose my underwear—I found God."

I tell him I see no big monk beard. I look at his clean-shaven face, his wrinkle-free long-sleeved, button-up shirt, with one button in the middle missed. There are a few stains on the pocket he cannot see, and I wonder how he irons his clothes.

"Yes, that was ten years ago. I do not want to die now. Before Jesus, my life was like the person with no food, and after eating, how that person feels. I was starving. I feel full. Now I am satisfied. I finished bachelor's in January. I started master's in classical Nepali literature. I will be only person in history of my village to have master's degree. I will go home and teach."

I tell him I bet his parents never saw that future for him.

"My father astrologist. Hindu fortune-teller. He write people's future on paper for them when they are child."

"What was the fortune he wrote for you?"

"None for me. No write, no paper, because they think no future. But on my father's horoscope from when he was a child, a man wrote: 'One of your sons will be wealthy, righteous, very much wise, very much educated.'" And he grins. "God gave me destiny, future. God had paper fortune written already." Ganesh bobs his head to the side, a sign of benediction.

Our children will also serve Him.
Future generations will hear
about the wonders of the Lord.
Psalms 22:30 NLT

Movements

Rick

S ome of us have experienced what we might call a revival, but revivals are not movements. Revivals happen when we return to something we have lost, but movements are not a return to anything—they are fresh beginnings. The civil rights movement in America, for example, represented a fundamental shift in people's thinking and a movement toward a political and social ideology that permanently changed the United States for the better.

In the church true revivals are rare, but movements are rarer still. Few of us will ever witness one. Revivals occur when Christianized people who have drifted away from their spiritual moorings swing back toward genuine repentance and sincere faith. Movements occur when a mass of unreached and unchurched people embrace Christianity. These first-generation believers have a different sort of faith than most of us will ever know. Their faith is less sophisticated, but more genuine.

Their communities, and especially their family members, often persecute them. They are susceptible to false doctrine, but they pray often and they give recklessly. They are tireless evangelists. They frequently witness miracles.

I wish I could say I discerned that a movement was about to begin in west Nepal when we first visited. I did not. Bev and I just happened to be at the right place at the right time, and through grace we enjoyed a rare privilege. But I did notice something unusual in those early days, and I realized that perhaps something wonderful could happen. There were frequent reports of extraordinary miracles, there were young believers who stood against heavy, sometimes violent, opposition, and there was an abandonment to worship and prayer in our little meetings that I had never seen anywhere, except in the underground church of China in the late 1980s.

Movements begin in opportunistic times. They are revolutionary and occur during upheaval and change. Though they are inspiring, they are also dangerous. They are unpredictable, unmanageable, and usually unexpected. Movements invariably bring division.

Movements challenge orthodoxy. Rapid change demands flexible structures and a creative mind-set. We quickly found ourselves desperate for leaders and turned to some of our capable women to help fill those leadership gaps. One of those women was Gita.

I first met Gita at one of our leadership meetings. We had organized a gathering of our village pastors and their wives in one of our main churches in Dang, a rice-growing region near the India border. Our churches in this area are filled with Tharu, an indigenous group that, until just a few years ago, was totally unreached.

She was organizing the line to a huge cauldron of biryani. We had about three hundred leaders gathered that day. She was an unusual Nepali woman, commanding and no-nonsense, with a bright, intelligent gaze. Seasoned pastors followed her direction like sheep to the watering trough. She scuttled about in a simple sari, directing traffic with well-defined cinnamon arms. On the back of her left hand, I spotted the remnants of a crude tattoo.

"Who is that woman?" I asked one of our leaders.

"That's Gita," he answered. "She's a former Maoist."

Her raw leadership temperament impressed me. Later in the day, when she came forward to give herself to a call to leadership, I remember speaking over her life about the Lord's plan for her.

She attended our training school that year and proved to be a capable leader. She was a little rough around the edges, but her faith was unshakable. She returned to her village to start a church and met immediate opposition from her relatives and the villagers. She was the only believer in that area, and none of them were impressed with her new faith.

She started her church with three women, and within a year the congregation had grown to about seventy-five adults. I visited her in her first year, and we sat in a tidy mud-walled church that looked like it would seat about fifty. The roof was thatch over hand-hewn timbers, and the floor, hard-packed earth.

"Nice building," I said.

"I built it myself," she answered.

It turns out she had literally built it by herself. With the three women who came to meetings in her home, she built a church on a piece of government land her community had squatted on. She cut trees from the jungle, shaped the timbers with an axe, dragged them out of the forest, placed them with the help of her female converts, and thatched the roof. The women dug mud and shaped the walls in the Tharu fashion, plastering the thick damp earth onto a grid made from bamboo and heavy reeds. The four of them started meeting to the ridicule of all the villagers. By the end of the year, her building was full.

In October 2016, I visited her again. Her church had grown to over 250. They met in a new building made from bricks that the church members kilned themselves. They couldn't afford to buy bricks, so Gita figured out how to build a kiln and took charge. The building is metal roofed, accurately squared, and has a concrete floor. The old mud building is still standing, but it's beginning to disintegrate.

"Why don't you tear that old building down?" I asked.

"It's a reminder to our people of what you can accomplish when you have faith," she said.

Gita is about thirty-five years old now. She told

me that she wants to remain celibate—that a husband would be too much of a distraction from her work. She has a bicycle and is starting churches in nearby villages. She has three so far.

Though her lifestyle is unique, her work is not. Something unexplainable has been happening among the Tharu people who live in the border region straddling Nepal and India. The Hindu system they lived under for more than three thousand years had enslaved them. They are beginning to understand that the gospel is a way to freedom—from religion, from cultural tyranny, and from economic slavery. The transformation has been rapid and astonishing.

About 20 percent of our leaders are women. A few are single, like Gita, but most of them are married. The work they do is astounding. In the past ten years, the Lord has helped us to plant nearly three hundred churches in Nepal, representing about twenty thousand believers. Over 98 percent of these believers are first-generation Christians coming out of Hindu and Buddhist backgrounds. They're becoming a force. We now have over ten thousand attending our annual gathering of the churches.

Many of these village churches have over two hundred believers; some of them are over five hundred. Entire villages are undergoing revolutionary change. In Gita's village the believers are helping one another build new homes from the bricks they make from their homegrown kiln. They even stamp the bricks with a Christian symbol. A village that ten years ago was a ramshackle cluster of mud homes is now an organized community.

The harvest field is producing multiplying leaders who are truly making a difference. We do not know what the future holds, but in this season the harvest is ripe.

Let me proclaim your power
to this new generation,
your mighty miracles
to all who come after me.
Psalms 71:18 NLT

GITA

Bev

Women carry heavy things on their heads. Men do not. Men carry heavy packs on their shoulders. Gita carries things on her shoulders. —Dinesh

Someone said before she was a Christian, she was a rebel leader in the Maoist uprising. I heard she went to war. I'm not sure if she fought, but it wouldn't surprise me. —Bikash

She tore down a house and carried it back to her village. —Kiran

The huge river near her house—one hundred meters wide—she swims it to go to church. I've seen her do it. She can bike faster than anyone too. —Amir

When she was sixteen, villages were trying to elect her as leader, and she wasn't even on the ballot. —Rajesh

He makes my feet
like the feet of a deer;
he causes me to stand on the heights.
He trains my hands for battle;
my arms can bend a bow of bronze.
Psalm 18:33–34 NIV

The village she built is serene—it looks like Tuscany. The sun sets over mustard flower covered hills. Timber thatch and brick houses nestle between flowering shade trees, which throw spots of sunlight on green, smooth grass. Lanky wildflowers crowd split-rail fences in bursts of color. The only sounds are the heavy metal scrape of a bucket against well walls, and a neighbor's bellowing cow.

She sculpted her farm from wilderness on the shoulder of a highway. Some of the traffic consists of bikes, motorcycles, and a few cars. Most of the traffic looks like living shrubbery, people carrying a bushel of some sort of plant, walking for miles to another village or to a market. The hills make the hectares slope at a slight downward angle. It is perfectly settled. Her land is nothing like the surrounding villages—all ochre-colored dirt and chaos, trash everywhere.

When people visit, the villagers throw flower petals into the air as they walk through the twine-bound reed gate. The locals decorate the visitors with necklaces of golden mums and purple thistle flowers from Gita's gardens. I look around among the faces for the legend as we make our way through the flower sprinkle, but I cannot find her. Everyone seems normal, not commanding, not like what I've heard about her. One woman is placing a flower garland on Rick's neck. She is thick, smiling, perhaps a grandmother. Another taller woman stands back and holds a baby; she looks too young. A third woman is looking into a pot, squatting in the dirt, eyeing dogs that are scooting closer to the food.

The two dogs appear to have nominated themselves as part of the village pack. It's clear that they are only grudgingly welcomed, but that they too have carved out an existence here. Nepal isn't kind to its dogs; most of them are bony and panting, lying in streets as speed bumps for cattle or motorcycles. They edge closer to what appears to be chicken curry. The woman hisses at them, quietly, through her teeth. One of the dogs emits a low growl and the woman leans forward, baring her teeth, ferocious with her taut cheekbones and big eyes. The dog simpers and drops his ears. She turns and catches my gaze. The woman's lips cover her bared teeth, and she bows her head. The dogs still wait for the bit of food they hope she will throw them. They must have sensed what anyone could sense about her despite her stern face—she cares. They haven't advanced, though; they also know everyone obeys her. I have found Gita.

She disappears as our group eats lunch, and when we walk outside, she is sitting on a small stool. She is thin, but not frail. Her skin stretches pleasantly over her bones—strong, knife-edged features—and she looks like a painting of a native warrior. She's not the smiling type. Her shoulders are slumped and she leans forward, her elbows resting on her knees, relaxed and apart, like a construction worker after a ten-hour day. Some Nepali women carry an umbrella for sun protection (light skin is their cultural ideal), but not Gita. From the stories I'd heard, I expected an ammunition pack and a host of rebel bodyguards. She has neither.

Gita was born in a place called the Village of Rivers. She has three sisters, and to her father's disappointment, no brothers. Daughters are not considered permanent family because they will eventually marry and move to their husbands' homes. Two of her sisters married and had children. But when Gita was young, her mother became sick and Gita decided not to marry when her father threatened to leave. "I said to my father, 'I will never marry and leave. I will serve you like a son, for all of your days and for all of mine.'" But her father left anyway. He adopted his nephew and moved in with him; he had found a son for himself.

Her mother had a weak constitution, constantly

suffering with different illnesses. There was one good hospital in their part of the country, and Gita wanted the best care for her mother. No witch doctor or guru could help her, no matter how much they paid or sacrificed. They had only a bike in their family, but Gita's mother was not strong enough to sit on the back rack while her daughter pedaled. "I decided she must go to hospital, so I carried her on my back to the hospital many times, many miles each way. Only sometimes we found a bus."

One night, after years of pain, Gita's mother called her into her room. She was close to dying. She took her daughter's hand and asked her to arrange a marriage for the youngest sister. Normally, this was the job of the father or brother, but Gita had taken their place. She promised her mother, who died later that night. Gita was twenty-four years old.

Gita slipped into a cadence of depression and duty. She was the guardian; she and her sister lived in her parents' old house, and she took care of her sister until she could arrange a marriage. She had given her life, her future, to care for her mother. She had no father who loved her, and her male cousins pressured her to move out of the house after her mother died. They reclaimed the house, and Gita moved to the town. She worked in someone's home as a servant, cleaning and cooking. She traded her strength and freedom for a roof and dal bhat. She trudged through the next few years.

"I felt alone. I had no friends. My family lived far

away. Washing and scrubbing and cooking times ran my day. I heard that my father died. I was twenty-seven years old. I knew I was too old to think of myself as an orphan, but that is how I felt. No one cared for me," she says. And she shifts on her stool, digging her toe into the dust. Just now she looks more like a child than the fable everyone's talking about.

Her sisters had families, but she felt she would burden them if she moved into their small mud houses. "I slept and ate and worked, and I dreaded each day that came. Why was life so long?" Gita continues looking at the ground, and her eyes stare in an unemotional, guarded way. A pocket of stale sadness hovers, in the way that scars are still evident on the skin, and it is impossible to ignore. "I had fulfilled my purpose of caring for my mother already. My purpose died with my mother."

In a moment, Gita shakes her head slowly, and when she blinks, the orphan disappears and the powerful woman reappears. "One day a woman in the town invited me to her church. I said I would go. Maybe she would be my friend, I thought." At church they asked her to become a Christian, but Gita said she needed to ask her older sister's advice about changing faiths. The pastor, Multilal, explained she didn't need to get advice, that she could talk to God directly. In her world, Multilal had been a guru of their faith, and she couldn't understand why he would so quickly give away the power of being the only one who heard God's voice.

Tharu people are animists—they see gods in everything, in nature, in earth. They don't have pastors; they have gurus. Gurus control everything because people are afraid of them. Anything that happens with crops, sickness, family disputes, the people go to the guru. They bring pigs, sheep, and goats and give money for a blood sacrifice.

"The gurus keep the precious meat to eat—they get fat from poor people's sacrifices—and they keep the money. Most times, guru prays, but our problems are still not solved," Gita says, and there is a glint of humor in her eyes. One side of her lip is turned up in a smirk.

Multilal was giving away his authority, Gita thought. He told her repeatedly that she didn't need a guru, that she could talk to God like he talked to God. "This was the God of the gods. I had never heard such good news," Gita says.

The woman who brought her to church brought Gita home with her afterward and fed her. They all fed her. The group spent time together, meeting in homes and talking. They asked about her life, and for the first time since her mother died, she had family. "In the Christian faith, I noticed they call each other 'brother' and 'sister,' and I really felt they were my brothers and sisters." Gita stammers through the last few words. She is crying, a bandana crumpled to her face. We pause for a moment, and a cow moos in the field nearby. Someone gets water from the well. She draws her breath again. "Soon I moved in with Christian family. They gave me strength. I had lost my mother and father, but God gave me spiritual family. I had new strength, new support."

As she was working and living in the town, she grew to know God, and her depression waned. She started to help people and started sharing her food and money. After a few months, she heard her nephew's cows were sick. His family depended on cows for their income. She was worried, so she borrowed a bike and rode the two miles to his house. She saw that they needed her help to survive, so every two days she rode her bike to his house and helped his family tend the cows. She shared what she'd learned about Jesus with them.

There was a big jungle on a stretch of highway she passed when she visited him, and she decided they should take over the land and build a house there. "This land," she says, and she motions around her, "it was terrible, useless land." They worked for months chopping down trees, filling in holes in the land, and building a new mud house for her nephew's family. They cleared a spot in the jungle and led his cows several miles down the road; they packed their possessions, and they moved into the new house.

Gita is talking about sick cows, and I start to shift in my seat. I decide to be direct in my questions. I want to know a bit more about her feats of strength, to see if what people say is true or if I can get the full story from her. I ask about the riots when young people in her village rebelled against the government. She stood between the young rebels and the police. She shrugs. "I was worried their futures would be ruined." She told the police they could arrest her if the young people ever rioted again, that she would take their punishment, and everyone agreed to these terms. "I turned to the group, and their ears rang with my words of warning. They respected me for saving them, and they gave me their loyalty and listened. They did not riot again." I ask if she considers herself a gang leader. She smiles and stares at the dirt.

Hearing some of the rumors proved true, I ask about another, more forward topic. The Maoists started to rebel in 1996. She'd been touted as a Maoist leader; the word *soldier* had even been bandied about. "I saw much fighting in the streets, the blood and war men make on each other. I said I did not want a part in that, even though they asked me to join their violent cause. But I always will help the hurt people, hungry people too. They offered me jobs, but I wouldn't take them. I continued to say I would not be a leader, but I also continued to serve in my village, to defend the weak ones who could not defend themselves. I was a leader, but in different way.

"When my father died, his house and land belonged to my sisters and me," she says, artfully changing the subject from Maoist leader to basic daughter. "Tharu tradition said we could not inherit the land because we were women. Nepali government said we had the right to inherit the land even though we were women. The two laws disagreed." In order to get the land and her father's house, her male cousins told everyone she was gone and had abandoned the home. The cousins moved in, and they exiled and threatened Gita. They told her they would kill her if she went home to take over her father's house.

I ask if she obeyed their orders, and she huffs. "For a little while," she says. She was happy, working hard, having a new Christian family, helping her nephew settle and prosper in the new land, when she decided she needed a house for herself. She wanted to reclaim her father's old home. It was a large timber structure with beautiful straight wood. She went home, and again her cousins threatened to kill her. She went to the police and filed a report with them. They divided the property in two, giving Gita only one-half of the land, and the other half of the land and the house to one of her cousins. Her cousin ignored the police and still threatened her.

"I don't need the house," Gita said she told the police. "He can have the house." All she asked for was help to get timbers from her father's land so she could build her own house. The police gave her cousin one month to get the timbers for her new house. One month passed, and her cousin never gave her the timber.

When she went back to her father's land, the guru was there making sacrifices for someone. She used to be afraid of the guru, begging him for her mother's health. "That day, I told the people in the village they didn't need the traveling guru anymore, that they could be connected directly to the most powerful guru of all."

Gita told the guru they did not need him to come to the village anymore, that they had a new guru. He agreed to stay away, but he warned the people not to touch the idols in the holy place. "Only she can touch the idols," he said to the villagers. "She is a Christian, so she will throw away the idols. These idols will not harm her, but they will kill anyone else."

"The people of the place, they noticed that I had the greater God. When the guru left, I went into the temple, and everyone was afraid. It was a small room, dark and filled with incense. I bent down to the idols—they were the size of my palm—and I put them all in a basket." Gita's face warms at the memory. "'See!' I told the crowd that had gathered. 'You made these—from dirt near your homes. What kind of god can you make? What god is formed of dirt? And what god can fit into a basket?'

"I threw an idol to the ground and it broke. 'What god can break?' I said. "The people stared. 'I know of an unbreakable God—the God who made dirt, who made the earth. He will make your life better. He is not scary. He is full of love. You can talk to Him without a sacrifice of blood.'"

Everyone was amazed she had not been harmed by the gods. People who had touched the gods before suffered psychotic episodes.

After her foray into god-breaking, she went to her cousin's house to take what was owed to her: timber. "I gave you one month. Now I am going to break my father's house," she told him. He did not believe her. She waited till everyone left for a day, and then she brought a machete. Climbing onto her father's roof, she hacked away the thatch, prying apart the boards and dismantling the timbers. She worked all day, until she heard her cousin yelling. Her cousin threatened to kill her.

"But I had a machete, so I turned from my work. 'No, today I will kill you. You did not help me. This is my timber you owe me. I'm taking it. Leave me to work.' That is what I said to him."

Gita doesn't look up from the ground. Everything she says she says matter-of-factly. She's in a house battle with machetes, and she's saying it like she's reading the grocery list aloud.

It took her several days to dismantle the roof and the walls. She decided she didn't want the other half of her father's land anymore; she wanted to live near her nephew and his family. After she'd gotten most of the structure removed, only the large support beams remained. She dug a trench around each beam and hauled pails of water from the well.

Carefully, all day, she worked on soaking the ground around the pillars. When the ground was soft, she attached a big rope to the top of the beam, wrapped it around a tree as a pulley, and leaned all of her strength into the rope until the beam came down. She brought the timber home, and eventually she had a house of her own near her nephew on the land she helped settle.

Soon after her house was built, she started to have church meetings there. She invited Multilal to preach whenever he could. Other times, she preached. Her nephews and nieces and their families started attending. She started with three people, but soon her church became too large for her house. She decided to build a church building on their land.

Most of the houses are mud houses, most made from tall sticks, timbers, and mud smeared against the sticks to stop wind and rain. But mud houses last only five years. She did not want to rebuild a big church in five years, so she decided she would need brick. She built the kiln.

"I cleared another spot in the jungle with a machete, felled logs, and chose long timber for the roof. We made bricks, and we smoothed the floor. Day by day we raised the walls as the bricks cooled, smearing mud between them as mortar. When we collected money, we would buy a bag of concrete to stucco the outside walls to protect them from rainwater in monsoon season," she says.

"Now we bake brick and work our way through

the Christian brothers and sisters, building each other new houses, one at a time. One day our village will be only brick homes. Many people who see our village tell us, 'We will not even work together to build a new temple. Our houses are bad. We are too greedy.' But they cannot unite to build together, to help others, because they are too worried about themselves. I tell them Jesus teaches us to worry about our neighbors, and in this way all of our neighbors are taken care of. I say all of the good things come to us because we are all thinking of giving—they are only thinking of receiving—and only good gifts come to you when you are giving. They do not understand, so they live in poverty and loneliness." When she is finished talking, Gita swipes her black bandana across her forehead, where beads of sweat have gathered. She folds and refolds the cloth, smoothing it across her knee.

Now Gita spends her days riding her bike to other towns, helping them set up churches of their own. She teaches them how to do what she has done in her village. People are free from their gurus, and people have spiritual families—she has fostered what she found. I ask her if it's true she is an excellent biker. She grins. "Everyone who rides with me has to stop, and then they take the bus," she says.

I'd noticed two tattoos on her hand when we first arrived: one was a cross and one was a black-smudged circle. I reach over and touched them gently, breaking the formal barrier between us. She explains that she'd had an OM symbol, the name of one of her old gods, Lord Shiva. When she became a Christian, she had it blacked out.

Gita was a devotee of Shiva for five years before she met God. "Each morning, I take a bath and then pour water on a stone in worship of Shiva." I tell her I don't even bathe every morning, and we laugh. Is Shiva the god of good hygiene? I ask her. "No," she says, and she smoothes her thumb over the tattoo. "He is the god of the dark. I was afraid if I didn't worship, Shiva would be angry. My spirit felt like evil wind."

Shiva, a main Hindu god, is depicted as bleak and violent, or blissful and wild—he is unstable. He is primarily known for darkness and unpredictability. He is much like the wheel of fortune; one moment your village wants you to be in charge, and in the next moment your parents are dead and you're homeless, reduced to being a bondservant.

"When I met Jesus, I ask myself how I thought watering rock could help me. It couldn't. I covered Shiva up. Then I got a cross." Christian tattoos are not normal in Nepal. She wasn't paying attention to what was normal; she just did what she wanted to do.

I ask her if she knows she is extraordinary, and if she's heard of the stories people tell about her. So far every tale people had told me was true, but she would give me only pieces of the narrative. "It has been 3,872 days ago since I became Christian.

People say I have done a lot in those days. I say I am just trying. Trying is all we can do," she says. "I'm not extraordinary. God is strong."

We are silent for a moment, and I turn in my seat to take in the setting sun and the gathering haze on the hills. Gita owns plenty of land;[30] she has so much responsibility for the village and the churches and even the churches that lie across the river she swims. I wonder aloud if she regrets never marrying, not having a mate. She doesn't answer at first. Finally, she breathes in slowly and sighs, and I regret asking my question. In the moment, I worry I've caused sorrow.

"In the nights," she begins, "when the men have gone to sleep, and the babies drool on their mothers' shoulders, and the water buffalo still need milking, the women sit around the fire. 'We wish that we would be like you,' they say to me." She laughs. "'You are living your good life,' they tell me. I did not get husband, and I did not get water buffalo, which burst without the milking and is sick too often. No, no. I do not regret. I have much family now."

She covers her head with her bandana, a cultural sign of humility and subservience. For the first time, I look at the bandana. It is like a silly prize from a carnival for throwing a ping-pong ball into a fishbowl. It's black and covered in blue lightning strikes. Proudly, at the center of the square, a muscled man is carrying some sort of a weapon. In English, around each side, the word *superhero* is written in all caps. She folds the fabric and places it on top of her bowed head as women in Nepal do before they pray. The bandana lies so that only the word *hero* is showing.

So each generation
should set its hope anew on God,
not forgetting his glorious miracles
and obeying his commands.
Psalms 78:7 NLT

DHANSING

Rick

For everything there is a season . . .
A time to cry and a time to laugh.
A time to grieve and a time to dance.
Ecclesiastes 3:1, 4 NLT

Dhansing is one of the young blind men I have helped in Nepal. His name does not mean "dancing," but to me he will always be a dancer. He's from a very remote area in the west, one of the least developed regions on earth.

I first met him in the predawn at Deepnath's house. He wore a light jacket that was not thick enough to ward off the chill. There was nothing attractive about him. His clothes were threadbare and faded. He could barely afford soap, much less deodorant. When I met him, I shook his hand and laid my left hand on his shoulder to let him know exactly where I was standing. His hand was cool, his grip tentative, and his shoulder thin.

I greeted him in English and he laughed, unaccustomed to my foreign speech. He tilted his head in the peculiar way that blind people do, looking at me from that space between his ear and his eye. His sunglasses, askew and greasy, reflected the dim glow of a cooking fire that burned just inside the home. The teapot boiled over, and he knew it before any of us. He said something in Nepali, and someone scrambled inside to lift the hissing kettle from the fire.

We had breakfast together—sweet water-buffalo-milk tea, hot barley naan with ghee, boiled potatoes. I asked him to tell us how he lost his sight.

When he was an infant, he had an infection in both eyes. There was no medical care in his valley. His parents took him to a village shaman who treated him by pouring hot oil mixed with herbs into his eyes. He lost his sight. As he told his story, one of the young Nepali men with us grew angry and said, "You should tell us who that man is. He must still be alive. He needs to be held accountable for what he did to you."

Dhansing leaned toward the young man who had spoken, found his arm and rested his hand there, and said quietly, "I've let it go."

It was stunning, and I fought back tears for quite a long time. This young blind man had accepted his past and truly forgiven his enemies. He had no bitterness. His life was beautiful.

Later that day we walked to the hostel where he lived with about thirty other blind children. The walk was not that long, maybe thirty minutes, but I fretted the whole way. Dhansing walked ahead of us, led by his friend Datta, who is what we would call legally blind. Datta has cataracts and can only see through a tiny window on the edge of his right eye. He peers at the world through that little portal, reading messages on his mobile phone from an inch away, scanning his path in quick, birdlike glances, greeting folk with a sideways gaze. I don't know how much he can see, but it can't be much. He stumbles often.

Dhansing held Datta's arm just above the elbow and walked a little behind and to the left. They led us along a single-track path that wound along the edge of a steep slope. We weren't in big mountains, but the drop-off to the left was at least a five-hundred-foot fall. The two blind men stumbled often, sometimes precariously near the edge of the trail. I followed closely behind, reaching for them every time they faltered. There were six of us traveling together, and the Nepalis ignored the stumbling blind men. After a while I realized Datta and Dhansing knew what they were doing, and I relaxed.

From behind the blind men, I began to appreciate their gait. They danced together over that rock-strewn path, sliding their feet along to sense the stones and guiding one another with subtle finger movements and shifts in their positions. They didn't cling to one another or grasp for support, and what at first appeared to be a halting manner was not that at all. They danced along that precarious path, their choreography as skillful as any I have seen on stage.

We provided for Dhansing for more than six

years. He finished his education, found a job teaching in a Nepali government school, rented a little village house, and married one of the girls in our blind children's home. He was twenty-one and she was nineteen when they married.

In a few months, they were pregnant. On November 5, 2013, Dhansing's wife, Pankali, gave birth to a beautiful six-pound, six-ounce little girl. I was anxious to see the child, hoping that her sight was all right. The baby was gorgeous. She had clear skin and bright eyes, and gazed with alert and normal vision. They asked me to name the baby, and with the help of my Nepali friends, I named her Rosanie—"guiding light."

It's difficult to describe how moving that experience was for me. I thought of how that beautiful, sighted little girl, even as a toddler, would lead her mother and father through life. I thought of her playing tricks on her mom, hiding as quiet as a mouse in the corner and moving things in the room. And I thought of that bittersweet day when Dhansing and Pankali would give their pair of eyes to a man who would take Rosanie as his wife, a sacrifice of love as in "The Gift of the Magi."[31]

I have received far more from Dhansing than I have given him. I have learned the beauty of letting go. To me, his name is *Dancing*.

People often feel sorry for me. I don't feel sorry for myself, but I have to admit that sometimes I use my handicap to my advantage. Datta and I once decided to travel to Nepalgunj to visit the church there. We had heard about it from Deepnath, but we wanted to see it for ourselves. At that time the road was very bad, and some sections were not yet built. It was at least a five-day journey for a sighted person. For us it would take even longer. And besides, we didn't have enough money for the bus fare from the market below Manma to Nepalgunj.

We walked to Jumla town, which took us a full day. Nepal was in a contested national election, and the United Nations had posted international monitors in the rural areas to make sure the Maoists did not intimidate voters. We heard that UN helicopters were making supply runs from the Jumla airport to Nepalgunj.

The helicopter was not there when we reached Jumla, so we sat at the airport and waited two days. We had only a little money, but some people there gave us some chapattis and some tea and a few eggs. On the third day, I heard the helicopter coming up the valley. It made deep thumping sounds, like the sound of a festival drum. I heard it for about five minutes before it reached us. When it landed, a strong wind hit us and blew my scarf away. The thumping stopped, and a high whining sound slowly dropped in pitch until all was quiet.

I heard the pilot tell the workers to unload the supplies as quickly as they could. The afternoon winds were picking up, and he wanted to return before the wind was too strong. He walked past us, and I knew he was going out of the security fence, probably to get tea. Datta and I waited until the men had unloaded the helicopter. When they passed us, it sounded like they were pushing a large wheeled cart. We waited a few more minutes, and I said to Datta, "Let's get on the helicopter."

We walked over to the machine and felt our way along its side. It was huge, much larger than I thought it would be. There was a big opening in the side, and we climbed in. We could not find any seats, so we sat on the floor in the back.

When the pilot returned, he said, "Hey! You guys get out of there!"

"We need to go to Nepalgunj," I said.

"Well, you can't go on this flight. This is an official UN helicopter. It's only for humanitarian work."

"We are blind," I said. "That is humanitarian work. And we need to go to Nepalgunj."

We argued with him for a few minutes, but he could see that we weren't going to leave the helicopter. Finally, he laughed and said, "Hold on tight. This will be a bumpy ride!"

I have never in my life heard such a roar, and when we lifted off, I felt strange, as if I were swinging in all directions at once. I got sick and threw up on the floor. Datta got sick too, but in about an hour, we were in Nepalgunj. The pilot said we shouldn't worry about the mess we made.

We have a very difficult life up in the mountains. I always felt that I was a burden to my family. I am strong, and even as a child, I did many things to help. I can cook and thresh rice and chop wood for the fire, but I cannot do much work in the field or find firewood or build a house. I've always been a burden to them. My family heard there was a blind hostel in our area where I could receive an education, and they took me there. We walked to the hostel in one day, but it was a very long day.

Foreigners from Europe supported the school, but they had never visited. The conditions were very bad. The stone house was broken, some of the walls with cracks large enough to put your hand through. It was very cold in winter, and we slept on mats on a dirt floor, huddled together to stay warm. There was not much food, and I was sick often. But they had Braille books and a teacher who taught us to read. I didn't care about my suffering. I was hungrier to learn than I was to eat.

I had been in the school for about five years when a foreigner came to visit us. He was an American, and everyone called him Pastor Rick. Not long after his visit, the Europeans who were helping the school stopped sending money. We all hoped that the American would help us.

We ran out of food, and about half of the children went home. I stayed and was about to give up hope when we received word that the church in Nepalgunj would help us. They sent us food, warm clothes, blankets, and even shoes.

Pastor Rick promised to build us a new home. I did not expect it to happen. I thought that by the time the house was completed, I would be finished with my schooling, but within two years, it was done.

It was a wonderful place, clean and large. It had indoor toilets and showers and running water, and after a year we had electricity. There was even a wood stove in the big room that we used in the winter to keep warm. I had never lived in such a nice place. People tell us it is the best building in our valley. A team of Tharu and Nepali men came from the Nepalgunj church to build it. They were very good workers.

Pastor Rick had asked us how we wanted the house built, and we all said we wanted cement floors and smooth walls. We told him we love smooth surfaces, as it makes it much easier for us to keep everything clean. He built it just like we asked.

I loved one of the girls in the school, but no one knew. Her name was Pankali. I knew she was beautiful because I overheard a woman in the village say, "Such a pretty girl. It's a shame she is blind."

I didn't care if she was pretty. I loved her because she was intelligent, and I loved her voice.

She did not sing like some of the other blind girls. Her voice was low, like a whisper, and not suited for song. But she spoke gracefully, and she laughed often. We were about the same age.

We sat alone one day warming ourselves in the morning sun. We had been talking, mostly about our studies, and I asked her if I could touch her. It was a very inappropriate thing to ask, and my heart was pounding so heavily that I could hardly hear her whispered answer. "I don't mind," she said.

I gently grazed the side of her face with my fingers. I could scarcely control my trembling. She was smooth, like the soft cool of the inner lining of a down-filled jacket. I thought to touch her lips, but I could not. My hand shook so much that I was afraid I would embarrass her. I pulled my fingers away and let the back of my hand trace lightly over her hair. It was indulgent, like the touch of warm rainwater.

She caught my hand and pressed her lips to my fingers, and I exhaled in an anxious sigh, my breath quivering as sweet and as skittish as the rise of a dove. When she released my hand, I lingered, grazing the side of her face again, and I felt the damp of a tear. We said nothing more, and we sat for a long while. From that day I noticed a change in her voice when she spoke to me. It was deeper, softer, more affectionate, and sometimes musical. The other students noticed it too and teased me. I did not care.

I did not have any money for a wedding, but a

couple in the Nepalgunj church invited us to join their wedding ceremony. We had a double wedding with music and food and much laughter. We even had a little room to stay in there on the church property. It was the happiest day of my life.

Life is such a mysterious thing. I have suffered much, but I have come to a place of contentment. I do not think much about those times when I suffered. If I were not blind, perhaps I would have never heard the message of the gospel. It has changed me. Perhaps I would never have had the opportunity for an education. Perhaps I would never have met Pankali.

We have a little girl now, Rosanie. She leads me about, clutching my index finger in her tiny little hand. She loves to sing to me. Sometimes, after she has had her bath, and she smells of lavender, and her hair is still wet, I hold her in my lap and tell her I love her. And she says, "I love you, too, Daddy." And I remember all the sadness, and the anger over my disability, and my disappointment, and my suffering, and I think that I have no regrets. I know who I am. I am Dhansing.

Then we your people,
the sheep of your pasture,
will thank you forever and ever,
praising your greatness
from generation to generation.
Psalms 79:13 NLT

SARAH AND DATTA

Bev

Many of the women in our Nepali churches wear the *tilaka*, a mark on their forehead that indicates they are married. It originates from the mystical Hindu concept of the third eye. Christian women usually don't wear it, but when their husbands are not believers, they have no choice. Many of them struggle to please their husbands, who are not at all happy that their wives are attending Christian services. We teach the women to serve their families in love, but in spite of their genuine efforts, there is conflict. Persecution is often the most severe in families. It's not pretty, and sometimes it proves to be an unbearable hardship.

On the other hand, our church members share a powerful camaraderie. Though the gospel has divided many Nepali families, it has also forged strong covenant bonds among the believers. They have a fellowship that few Westerners understand. Many of our believers are very poor, and some live at the precarious edge of survival. When poor Hindus or Buddhists accept the gospel, they risk their communities' protection and often their livelihoods. They sometimes lose their lands. They often lose their families.

In a land where marriages are arranged, the

divide between Christian and Hindu is a source of enormous conflict. How does a young female Christian convert reconcile with her Hindu family when they insist on finding a husband for her according to their traditions? Invariably, that choice will be a young Hindu man who will carry on the family's religious and cultural values. The young girls who live in the cities and towns often leave their families to live in a Christian home, but in the villages, that is usually impossible. When they are able to escape, their pastors take on the role of surrogate fathers and become actively involved in arranging marriages within the church family. Oftentimes it's a much more romantic process than we might think.

You have captured my heart,
my treasure, my bride.
You hold it hostage
with one glance of your eyes,
with a single jewel of your necklace.
Song of Solomon 4:9 NLT

The long wooden kitchen table was layered with plastic tablecloths and placemats. On one end was a bouquet of pink and white flowers that, seen out of my periphery for a few days, never seemed to die. After a week I wondered where the sumptuous garden was hiding that supplied these beauties. I leaned over and saw they were fake. They even had glitter-rimmed petals. I'd been tricked.

"Tharu art," Rick said. "The Tharu made that vase."

I hadn't noticed the vase, but I studied it now. It was made of kindergarten craft materials—the plastic graph with squared holes you'd use to make a shag rug of a unicorn for your mom's birthday gift. But they'd used it to cross-stitch hot-pink and green yarn into patterns, using seed pearls and shells to embellish it. Then they'd stitched the pieces together to form a vase. It was unique, and in a country where necessity is king and work rules the day, this small piece of art was precious and rare. Someone had skipped laundry, skipped a meal, stayed up into the night to make this for this table.

We'd just finished a church conference where ten thousand people descended from all over Nepal. They led goats, carried wire-trap cages full of chickens, and balanced thirty-pound bags of rice on their heads as they walked and bussed and biked to Nepalgunj. When they arrived, each tribe set up their own makeshift kitchen, and the appointed tribe "chefs" began their preparations to cook for the four-day conference for their group. They stacked bricks in a triangle, leaving the middle open to build a fire. Some poured water into the dirt and made mud, smearing it on the bottom of their pots so they could wash the soot off more easily after cooking. The pots were the size of kettledrums, and day and night, in sweltering heat, the camp chefs tossed and stirred dal bhat, with a musical, percussive insistence.

It was easy to see the differences among the tribes. They had their separate ways of dressing: some wore saris, and others wore harem pants and tunics. Americans have cooked together for so long they've developed a muddled multiethnic look, but Nepalis are distinct. Some appear to be the product of the blending borders with China or Tibet. Others have obvious traces of Indian. Because Nepal is communal and agriculture rich but cash poor, trade is tough, and transportation within Nepal is difficult. Most individual provinces still maintain identifiable physical distinctions.

During the conference, each group did their traditional cultural dance. Some wore peacock feathers on their head. Others did impressive dances with percussion sticks. But there was one group that stood out, and it didn't take long to identify them—the Tharu.

The Tharu wore the boldest colors at the conference. They have dark skin, high cheekbones, and black almond-shaped eyes. The Tharu dance team came on stage. The men wore button-up shirts with black pants, but the women wore bright traditional clothing and carried baskets the size of car tires on their hips. After the music started, they balanced the baskets on their heads for the entire dance.

Tharus take months to make the baskets. First, they sickle the grass, then let it dry. After it dries, they soak the reeds in dye for six weeks before weaving them into intricately patterned baskets. The baskets are impressive, but the most beautiful aspect is the rims. Women wade into the rivers and wetlands and pull thumbnail-sized shells out of the mud on the banks. They pry them open, scrape out the living mussel, and poke holes in the thickest part of the shell. Then they weave the shells into yarn, thread, tinsel, and whatever they can find and create a cascading curtain around the rim of the basket.

The Tharu are an indigenous group in Nepal, and they live in an area called the Terai. It's a patchwork quilt of grasses and grains, a canvas, of bold chartreuse, shocking yellow, and tropical lime, dotted with sky-mirroring wetland lakes. The air is even illuminated by the sun, vellumed by golden misting humidity and smoke from burning crops during harvest time. People are always in those Terai fields, wearing their bold reds and pinks and purples. Crowned with their raven hair, they squat and tend the crops, or find shade under banana trees with feathered leaves. In her electric-blue kurta, a woman wields a sickle in broad, sweeping strokes, and tall golden stalks of grass fall before her. It would be a painterly scene, if the Tharu story weren't so heartbreaking. It's a familiar tale of a tragic slide into slavery and the slow climb back to equality.

The Tharu build their homes from soil and reeds, which gives the village a copy-paste look, tans on tans. They bind the sickled grass into sheaves and weave it to make roofs. In the night against the blue, glowing sky, their raised haystacks take on a life of their own, black looming shadows.

Tharus are known for their malarial antibodies; they cannot acquire the parasite, despite the warm mosquito-infested lands they live in. Their strong family connections, the fertile food-rich forests, and their malaria-dodging ability meant that for generations they controlled the Terai. The Tharu were largely untouched until the 1950s, when the World Health Organization declared a war on malaria in the area. Once the deadly virus was gone, outlanders moved in to the lowlands and enslaved the Tharu. For fifty years the Tharu were bondservants. Only recently has this changed.

At the end of the church conference, the Nepali pastors called my group, the Westerners, onto the stage. At the end of the ceremony, they handed me a small basket of woven pinks and greens, with a shell curtain cascading from the rim to the base. They use whatever materials they can find to embellish the baskets, and mine had silver plastic drinking straws, bound in tiny triangle spikes around the edge.

Sarah is a Tharu. She is at the door of the

kitchen, and her husband is beside her. I see her glance at the Tharu vase. She looks into my eyes and smiles, then meekly reaches out to place her hand on Datta's arm, lightly signaling him in the way married couples do. He is squinting; he is 90 percent blind. He reads her signal and sidesteps, missing hitting his shoulder on the doorframe. She guides him without words, and from their proximity and warmth with each other, in a moment I see she has worked to keep his dignity. Datta sits, and she walks around to take the chair next to him. Datta is small, but Sarah is smaller. His shoulders are sloped, but not in defeat; he has the posture of contentment, confidence, and relaxation. Sarah's shoulders are square and strong, and though her clothes are loose, I can see the curve of her muscles. She is nervous; she is a housewife and worker—she has never been interviewed before. But Datta takes her hand under the table, and she breathes and relaxes, turning her knees towards him.

In America personality is king and charisma is social currency. Sarah and Datta are quieter. They value humility. Their personalities are subtle. At first, being with them is like being in a noise vacuum. After some time I can feel the gentle undercurrent in the room, the subtle communication. It's like the difference between an electric guitar and a harp, between a water park and a bubbling spring. It's like being aware of a low ceiling or listening for a murmur. She bows her head and whispers to him.

He leans in to her; they are in constant contact with each other. They are obviously deeply in love.

I ask how she spells her name.

"It is only written in Nepali, never in English," she says. Nepali writing looks like hieroglyphics. "There are no letters yet."

And in that moment, I'm left with the responsibility of writing her name for the first time in English, and choosing whether she gets an *H* on the end, or if I should leave it with just an *A*. I decide an *A* is a pointy letter, with a jarring sound. It is *arithmetic, alimony*. *H* has a soft sound. It is sometimes silent. *H* is humble, honest. It is the sound of a laugh, a "ha ha." *H* requires an exhale, a breath, and Sarah is just that—she is a pause, white space on a busy page. "S-A-R-A-H," I tell her.

I ask if they want any Coke. I've already poured a little for myself.

"No," she demurs. She looks down and tips her chin towards her chest. She wears hot pink, and I am beginning to think it is the national color of Nepal; it is everywhere.

I don't drink Coke at home, but in Nepal it's almost impossible to resist. I ask what a treat is for them.

"My people eat *ghonghi*," she says, and from the way her eyes crinkle and glitter, I know she wants me to ask the next obvious question.

"What is ghonghi?" I oblige.

"You call it a snail." She smiles big. She knows

it's not something Westerners eat, and as I shake my head, we both giggle. It is a light joke, but in Nepali gentleness, it's the height of humor.

Sarah grew up in poverty, with five siblings in a small, two-room house. Her family was Hindu and Tharu, both of which leave little room for advancement, with both adhering to unspoken caste systems. She attended school until she was eight, dropping out to help with the arduous task of farming for a poor family of seven. At seventeen years old, Sarah took a break from her farming duties and traveled to Nepalgunj with her Christian aunt, who took her to church. "Before that, I did not have life. I wanted to die. I thought there was no purpose for me." After she became a Christian, Sarah began making regular trips to Nepalgunj to spend time with other believers. Her countenance changed, her purpose changed, and peace and happiness became her hallmark. I ask if she met Datta in church.

"Not for a long time; he is from Jumla. My pastor, Sushila, called me to the kitchen one day. I was twenty. She was standing with Datta," Sarah says. I look at Datta and watch his smile grow. Sarah looks at his smile and makes the first syllable of a gentle laugh. "Sushila told me Datta is a good man, and to pray, and if I wanted to, I could marry him."

So this was an arranged marriage. I had only heard of arranged marriage in the form of forbidden love and jail-sentence-like engagements. Before coming to Nepal, my idea of arranged marriage was negative. I had pictures in my mind of weeping brides, forceful husbands, greedy parents.

"People suggested three men to me. My father offered me a Hindu man, and Sushila offered me one other man and then Datta."

I was curious who was up against Datta in the race for a wife.

"He was a businessman. Christian, working man. Living here. Nice man," she says.

Arranged marriage sounded more like a dating service than what I'd expected. The elders make suggestions based on the subjects' personality types, financial status, societal status, and physical attributes. They think of far more things than Westerners do when considering a mate. But even given the choice, Sarah chose a blind man whom she had not spent time with, who lived in Jumla in freezing temperatures every winter. The other marriage proposal probably offered the opportunity to be a housewife to a fully able-bodied man in a city near the Terai in an environment closer to her childhood home.

I ask why she chose Datta. He turns his head towards Sarah, squeezing her hand. But after spending only five minutes with Datta, I already know the answer. "He is kind. A good man. Strong. I had a dream about him where I saw him loving people, talking about God to them, and serving them; and when I woke, I knew I wanted to marry him. I told Sushila, and nine days later we had our wedding."

I ask her if she was nervous to marry, especially

in such a short time, and she assures me she was not. "I never thought I would have a wedding like the church gave me. They are like family. I would never have had money for something so special." The church threw a sumptuous feast, and she wore a white sari. Her hair was washed, braided, and scented for the day, and the ladies put a touch of makeup on her clear cinnamon skin. It was a day she could never have afforded. It was luxurious, extravagant. "I felt like a queen."

The couple deliberates about the date of their anniversary. Though she hesitates, he is definite in his answer. He cannot hide his joy. "He knows," I say to her. "It was the day his heart grew brighter."

I watch as he smiles again. He says it softly, with great care: "Yes."

I think of the verse I found in Song of Songs when I was a young girl. It shocked me when I saw it then, but now I see it in Datta's demeanor. In the biblical story, King Solomon is crowned, and they call his wedding day the day of his heart's rejoicing. I remember being surprised at that verse; I'd always heard the wedding day called the bride's day. Certainly Sarah was happy, but there is a deep, effusive, joyful residue still glowing on Datta's face. "Light came to me on that day," he says. When he tells me the date the words fill with tenderness.

When watching Nepali talk about their affection, there is much demurring, blushing, shrinking back. It is not a topic often discussed—love. Datta and Sarah's soft touches, the unspoken physical contact that passes between them makes it obvious to everyone that they are in love. I had been in Nepal many times, and people still had to tell me who was married and who was related; it was not obvious from their physical affection. Women have traditional roles in the kitchen; men have traditional roles in the field. Both strive for survival; neither has time for dating, flowers, cuddles, and chocolates. In more time-honored tribal areas, women and men may not eat together or walk together, and fathers will not touch their children in public. Tenderness is not common.

Immediately after their wedding, Sarah and Datta left for Jumla—Datta, back to his life, and Sarah, to a world she knew nothing about.

Datta begins to explain Jumla. "I was born in a remote place with lots of hills, lots of troubles, and lots of difficult circumstances."

Most people in Jumla are illiterate, and they lack roads, food, water, schooling, and other basic government provisions. In the dry season, the land is desert. It's fractured ground, striated onto mountainsides, baked into plaques where it's a plain, and pimpled with pebbles and scrub plants. The homes are compact rectangles wedged into nooks in the hills. It appears that for every flat space the width of a man lying down, a family raised four dirt walls and called it a home. Years of sun and snow have expanded and contracted the mud and rock into steadfast compounds, and the homes, after several generations, look hammered into the hillsides. People farm wheat and barley; buy and sell buffalo, sheep, and goats; and sometimes travel to India in the summer to sell their livestock.

In the winter Jumla becomes what people would expect in the Himalayan foothills. Howling winds hover near zero degrees Fahrenheit, and the already infertile ground freezes. Snow piles up, and tiny drifts accumulate on windowsills and blow into homes. The people's dirt floors freeze into slippery surfaces with the evening frost and thaw into mush with the morning fires. People's hope and life-saving fat reserves ebb with the season, and if they have worked and stored enough food and firewood, they can survive.

It's no wonder they worship many gods. They look within their meager lives, meager existence with one pot, one stream a mile away, one goat, and a tiny plot of farmland where one rain can destroy or make a harvest. One episode of hail can drive a man to either suicide or starvation, two sides of the same dark dealing from their perceived god. They search to find the turnkey god of the hundreds of millions of Hindu gods, the one who can help them. Begging the god of rain, god of sun, of wheat, agriculture, fertility, hail, and pestilence gives them a sense of control over their destiny, their year. It's the only thing they can do, other than the little time it takes to tend their plots, to help. We all feel better with gods on our side.

And even if it rains too long, or it doesn't rain at all, the people have made their sacrifices. It is their way of holding out hope for as long as they can. They wait for a rescue, a deus ex machina,[32] a dénouement. But when the sun bakes their fields dry, or they wake up to a silvery sheen, crisp across their unripe crops, it is the worst and maybe the last day of their lives. The men make their way to a mountain cliff and jump. Sometimes they buy drink with their last few rupees, and they give up. Whether their god has failed them, or they have failed to please their god, they do not know. And if the gods aren't in the rescuing business, they feel their merciless lives aren't worth the dirty daylong striving.

"It is very hard for people to live. They have to work for a full twelve months to stay alive. Even if they worked every day for twelve months, it would be hard to fulfill their basic needs," Datta says. "Being blind there was difficult. I was sick in my eyes at five years old, and my parents took me to witch doctors to heal me, but they could not fix it. No doctors, no hospital. They used oils, different medicines, sacrifices, but I was fully blind by ten years old."

Datta's family is illiterate. When he became blind and could not work with the family in the gardens, he was useless to them, which freed him up to attend the local blind school. In year seven, he met Deepnath, a Christian pastor, and he became a Christian.

I ask Datta what changed for him after he became a Christian. It seems to me that being blind in a difficult place to live would make life hard enough. Becoming a Christian in a Hindu world wouldn't be a wise decision, and he must have been deeply affected and compelled in order to change faiths.

"After I meet Jesus, my life change." He describes how he only saw darkness for ten years and had to be led everywhere. He couldn't see anything and was at the mercy of someone else's help for everything. "My vision slowly improved. I can now see some light, and I can walk by myself where I need to go because I can tell shapes."

Datta graduated from the blind school a few years after he became a Christian, and he was so affected by his faith that he moved to the place where Deepnath found God, Nepalgunj. Datta attended Bible school there, and when he finished, his pastors asked him to go back to Jumla. The blind school in Jumla had a hostel, but it was full and not in good working order. The church would build a hostel for the students, and Datta could live there, teach at the school, take care of the children, and manage the hostel. He gladly accepted. And then a few years later, Sushila called and asked if he would like to be married. He said yes, and for two months he lay in bed at night, hoping she would find a wife for him. I asked him if he ever thought he would get married.

"It was out of my imagination. People would look at me and think it was a bad idea to marry their daughter to me. How would I feed or take care of her? No father wants that for his child," he says, and he shakes his head, a gesture blind people normally don't do because they can't see others and can't mimic their body language.

My favorite part of the whole conversation is watching Datta smile as he talks about Sarah. I tell Datta he is like a lightbulb switched on every time she is the subject. I am rewarded with the same high-wattage glow.

Their affection wasn't immediate; the union was arranged, but it was also voluntary. They were not in love originally, in the traditional sense. They had mutual respect, but they say it took about two months to become comfortable with each other, and in simple ways they began to connect—a shared cup of buffalo-milk tea, a brush of the hand while setting the table. It is far from what a Westerner imagines as romance, but in the simple, stripped-down existence of a Himalayan winter, survival calls for closeness for warmth, and Sarah and Datta huddled together into affection. At some point, neither remembers when, they told each other they loved each other. Their love was based on common goals: build the organization, help the blind children, help each other. Neither was looking to benefit from the relationship; the benefits happened naturally as each served the other and delighted in being loved fully. In loving each other, in learning each other, they've been surprised at what they've gotten in return for the gift of their service.

I ask if they have ever regretted being married, but I am mostly asking Sarah.

"Yes, but not because of Datta." Sarah is nervous about the question. She reiterates, four or five times, that she was happy with her husband, but the circumstances were difficult. "The blind kids hated me for a long time. They blamed me for everything wrong. They hit me and try to beat me and get us removed from the hostel. I was very sad then. And I felt maybe I was not worthy to serve them."

This woman left her home, her tropical climate, her family, and rich food to move to a poor mountain community to take care of a blind husband and seventeen blind children. And she felt not worthy? To me, at only twenty-three Sarah is not that far off Mother Teresa's trajectory.

"It took a long time to get them to be okay with me," she says.

I ask her what changed the situation, and she explains how some of the older blind children organized a coup because they wanted Datta's respectable position as head of the hostel. They complained to the government that the hostel wasn't being run appropriately.

When the inspector visited, he told Datta and

Sarah, "I see the problem here. You've ruined these kids. The home is new, the food is excellent. They are spoiled."

So Sarah kept serving, kept loving, cleaning, cooking, and working nonstop to make sure the blind kids were comfortable. She understood they had been badly abused and mistreated and they were angry. Her service and love were a consistent force in their lives, and eventually, after a year, they accepted her.

"What do you like about your husband?" This is a Westerner kind of question, and when I see her blush, I tell her that I don't mean to embarrass her. Gooey marshmallow love isn't the typical topic of conversation, and they don't have time or desire for romance stories. Their idea of love isn't troubadour-affected like mine is.

"He is kind person. He takes good care of me." She tells me at some point, a year ago, she was very sick. She developed a fever. When she brings up this part of the story, she melts a little into her seat, and she tells me a bride's secret: "He cooks for me when I am sick." It is shameful for a man to cook and clean in their culture. Datta does not care; he has lived his shame through his sickness and come through ridicule. He helps her in any spare time he has. Societal hierarchy is strong, gender roles chiseled into millennia of stone, but Datta ignores custom; Sarah's company outweighs the shame. He can hear the telltale small liquid pops as her lips separate and spread and she smiles, and he leans over to her face to see, and that is worthy of the extra work for him.

For the first time in our conversation, she volunteers more information. "He is strong. Whatever conditions, he never stops being kind and strong. He never quits."

"And Datta . . ." I turn to him and think I'm pushing my luck, asking a Nepali man, even a sweet one, to talk about how he feels about his wife.

"She is always walking by my side." He could have stopped with this statement; it says everything he wants. In Nepal a woman is supposed to walk behind her husband; it is tradition. It shows that the man is in charge. But Datta, even though he can see enough to walk by himself, wants his wife as close as possible.

"Everything has changed for me. Before, I was leading the school on my own, teaching and cleaning and praying on my own. Now we share responsibility. Every day it is good with her," he says. He describes how they garden together in the summer and how he asks for her suggestions in his work as a teacher because he values her opinions.

"But she never makes me feel like I am lower." Datta takes the conversation deeper. He's still thinking about what else he loves about his wife, not just how she helps him, but how she values him. "I am blind. She doesn't treat me like I am sick. She treats me like a man." Sarah enables his dignity. "And she waits for me. She cooks, and everyone else at the hostel eats. But she waits to eat with me when I get home from work." Some traditional Nepali men won't eat with their wives because it is shameful to not be served as head of the household, but Datta says it is his favorite part of the day.

These people go their whole lives and do not swap stories with anyone, maybe not even with each other. But Sarah is forthcoming again. "Whenever he goes to a city, he will bring gift for me. I like meat, so he will sometimes bring chicken. I don't have to ask. He will just bring it. And he buys me clothes."

Her hand goes to her neck, and she bends her head to look at the ornate gold chain there, a cross dangling in the middle. "This," she says simply, and her eyes fill with tears. She does not look up; it would be too intimate for her. "Very special." For years Datta saved a few coins at a time until he could purchase the luxury of a piece of jewelry for her; every cent they had went towards food, clothes, and keeping warm in the winters.

I ask if Datta could give any gift in the whole world to Sarah, what he would give her. I marvel at what these people have found in each other. My question seems brash, bold, and big. They are simple, and they've nurtured love in an impossible climate, against all odds.

"We have enough. We are happy. But I would build her a small house—her own house."

"Sarah?" I turn to her, and her eyes dart to the side. I sense eye contact is too much for what she is about to share, so I look at the tablecloth to find and refold my napkin to give her emotional space. She has already shared so much with me, and I don't want to push, to be crass in my questions.

"A baby," she says. And now I understand why she had been sick, why he'd taken care of her; they knew the heartbreak of losing a child. Sarah was four months pregnant when she went into early labor and miscarried. "He loves children. It would be the greatest gift. I hope . . ." and she stops.

Datta speaks again, still thinking of things he loves about his wife. I had asked about Jumla's rough conditions, and he told me that Sarah is strong. I had asked about how difficult it is for a blind man to run a school and a hostel for blind children, and he talked about Sarah's service. "She is very loving, and she takes care of me. When I come home every day, she comes to the door, greets me, and smiles."

For the Lord is good.
His unfailing love continues forever,
and his faithfulness continues
to each generation.
Psalms 100:5 NLT

PRAHALAD

Rick

We sat cross-legged on the floor and shared several cups of tea and a plate of cookies. Prahalad is a dark, strong fellow with a mouthful of large crooked teeth. Though he is in his fifties, he still looks like a brawler: strong hands, broad shoulders, lean torso, piercing eyes. But he is not at all intimidating. He has a bright, kind face, and he looks directly at you when he talks. He talks a lot. Passionate words spill out of him; he needs no prompting to tell his story. I liked him instantly.

Prahalad looks rough, but as soon as you make eye contact, you realize he is one of the beautiful people—a man who was once proud, then humbled, then rebuilt into something he never dreamed he could be. His wife beamed as he spoke, admiring him.

There were parts of his story that visibly shamed him. His enthusiasm would drop a few notches, and he would pause between sentences. He seemed to be reliving his regrets. I thought to ask him about regret, then changed my mind. Somehow, it just didn't matter what he had done or whom he had hurt or what regrets still lingered. He was trying hard to make things right. There was a quality about him that took me awhile to identify, but as he talked it came to me. He was grateful.

> *At that moment*
> *their eyes were opened,*
> *and they suddenly felt shame*
> *at their nakedness.*
> Genesis 3:7 NLT

Nine years ago, I was given a diagnosis that I was HIV positive. The clinic told me to tell everyone I had TB, but I knew the truth. I thought I would die. The doctor thought so too. He told me I would die quickly, gave me three weeks, and sent me to a hospice.

I had no hope. My world was darkness. I had no expectation, nothing but regret and sadness. I was ashamed of the things I had done. My wife received the same HIV test results, and though she was not yet sick, I knew that she would be. I was ashamed of what I had done to her. I wished a thousand times I could go back and do things differently.

I had been a proud man, and strong, but I was reduced to skin and bone. There was hardly any flesh on my body. I did not much care how I looked or how sick I was. I felt unwell, yes, but more than that, I was crushed under a burden of shame. I could not look my wife in the eye or meet my family members' gazes. I wept constantly, and I bore my shame without dignity. There was no dignity to the end I was facing—only regret, and sorrow, and humiliation. I did not deserve to live.

My son had become a Christian before I grew ill. When he had announced it to the family, I did not much care one way or another. Some of our family members were angry with him, but I said, "He is an adult now; let him make his own decisions."

I was not against the Christians, but neither was I for them. I just didn't care. I wanted to enjoy my life. I was not afraid to fight, but I didn't see the point. Fighting was something that came naturally for me, but I only fought when I was provoked. My son was not hurting anyone.

When I was younger, a policeman came to my village and tried to seduce my sister. He used filthy language with her and embarrassed her in front of our neighbors. What he did was shameful to us all.

"You should not disrespect my family like this," I said.

"Don't you know who I am?" he asked.

"I know who you are, but if you keep speaking to my sister in this way, I will teach you some manners."

He hit me in the face, and I spun away from him from the force of the blow. I had confronted him in the courtyard of my home. There was a small stool near the front door that had overturned while we were arguing. As I whirled away from him, I reached down and took hold of the stool's leg. I continued my spin, and when I came around, I caught him right in the jaw with the edge of the stool. He went down, and I beat him with that stool until it had broken into little pieces and there was nothing left to beat him with. He went back to his police station with a bloodied face, a broken nose, and a few teeth missing.

After a while four policemen came and told me I had to go with them to the police station. When I got there, they set upon me with truncheons. Even though they were armed, I could have beaten one or two of them, but four were too many. I fought as best I could, and I bloodied one of them, but they got the best of me. They beat me until I was unconscious.

A local politician heard about what happened, and he filed a case against the policemen. It took three years, but we won the case and the policemen were ordered to pay a fine. Before the case was finalized, they visited me and said, "If you drop the case against us, we will give you a job as a policeman."

"This is a dog's job," I said. "I will never do such work as this."

That's the kind of man I was—proud and arrogant and strong. But when I got sick, and I knew that my sickness was because of my sin, I was no longer proud. I was ashamed and humiliated. Even before I became a Christian, I knew that I had sinned. My disease was karma. I had sinned against God and against my wife and my children. I could bear my shame, but the shame of the suffering I caused to the innocent was too much. I thought I wanted to die, but later, when death drew near, I was afraid to die.

I let myself get very sick before I sought medical help. I thought I could push through it. But maybe, too, I felt I deserved the sickness. I really don't know. I had a good job in India as a manager in a factory. I spent most of the year there. It was in India that I got my disease. I kept trying to work, but I eventually reached the point where I could work no longer. I came home, and I wasted away in our little house in the village.

We were in a pitiful condition. I had never really cared well for my wife and family. We had a small piece of land and a mud house with a thatch roof. I grew so weak that I could no longer keep it repaired. My wife started getting sick as well and was too feeble to tend the garden or repair our home. When the monsoons came, our house crumbled around us. After the rains it was only partially standing. You could see through it; when it rained, we got wet. It was a difficult life. Most of the villagers thought we were cursed. We were cursed, but I was the only one who knew why. I began to get depressed.

I owed some money to a man in the village, and

he caught me one day at the well. He held me by my throat and demanded what I owed. I suppose he could see that I would not live much longer, and he wanted to get his money before I died. While he was shouting at me, I thought to myself, that if I were younger, I would thrash him to the ground for insulting me this way. But I was no longer young and I was no longer strong. I fell to my knees in front of him, and I began to weep. I begged him to give me time. I told him I would repay him everything.

He just looked at me. There was no compassion in his eyes, only contempt. I could tell he wanted to hit me, but I was so pitiful that he knew it was useless. I will never forget the humiliation of that moment. I was nothing to him or anyone else. In a village of people so poor the village did not appear on a map, I was the lowest of them all. I was a sick and sniveling dog, not even worth kicking.

When I reached the point where I could scarcely walk, I went to Nepalgunj to see the doctor. That's when I was told that I would die. That's when I was sent to the hospice. That's when my life ended, and when my life began again.

My son told my story to his pastor, Kali Basel, and he came to visit me. I was so weak that I could scarcely speak. All I could do was cry. I wept shamelessly before him. I had never felt so broken.

"Why are you weeping?" KB asked.

"I don't want to die."

"Who told you that you would die?"

I told him everything.

"What is the purpose of your life? What are you going to do?" he asked.

"I don't know. I don't want to die."

"Forget this word," he said. "You are not going to die. You are going to give hope to many people. God is going to use you powerfully. Will you give your life to serve the Lord?"

I wept bitterly and said, "My life is not worth saving. I am nothing."

"There are many people who are in your place. They are just like you. You are going to help them. Many miracles will happen in your life. You will heal many people."

He prayed for me, and I felt that this was a very significant moment. I had lost hope, but there was such a strong presence then. For the first time in my life, I felt that God would help me. I felt something very unusual in his prayer.

"If God heals me," I said, "I will serve Him with all my heart, and all my strength, and all my mind."

"Don't forget this promise," KB said. "And don't forget this word I have spoken over you."

After KB prayed, I felt as if light had come into my life, as if my eyes had been opened. I didn't know anything about the Lord, but my son began to visit me and teach me. Pastor KB came to visit from time to time. Within a month I felt strong enough to attend the church.

The doctors were amazed at my recovery.

Everyone at the hospice said it was a miracle. One of the church leaders was a Tharu like me, Pastor Mohan. He spoke my language and came to see me often. He prayed for me every time he visited, and he prayed for many people there in the hospice.

I gave my life to prayer and to reading the New Testament the Christians had given me. I did nothing else. I prayed, I read, and I taught others in the hospice what I was learning. Within two months the doctors sent me home. They gave me medicine to take, three tablets, which I took every day for the next nine months. I suppose those medicines helped me recover, but even the doctors said the medicine was not enough to heal me. They knew that something supernatural had taken place. The people at the hospice were spreading my story everywhere, even the doctors. Everyone knew it was a miracle.

When I returned to my village, the people were amazed. They didn't know what to say. I had been a womanizer, a drunkard, and an alcoholic. I had abused many of them. When I left, just a few months before, I was a wasted man. Everyone thought I would die. I returned healthy and strong and in my right mind. I became an attraction in the village. People would come and sit at my house and I would tell them my story, and they would ask me to pray for them. There were so many healing miracles that I cannot count them all: an epileptic healed, many women healed of issues of blood, people healed from migraines, fevers, stomach ailments, even cancer.

There was a little girl, only eight years old, who had cancer in her throat. She had an open wound that was hideous. Her family had taken her to the hospital in Chitwan and spent every rupee they had for her treatment. The treatment didn't work, and she was about to die. After we prayed, she began to improve. Now she is fine. Her entire family is in my church. Her father is working abroad and making good money. He had tried to send her abroad for her treatment, but now it's not necessary. Now he is the one who is abroad, and God is blessing them.

My life has completely changed. People think I am wealthy. I have a motorcycle, I pastor a church, and I have a farm that is producing good crops. I have two oxen, chickens, goats, and sheep. I dug a bore well, and it produces water without a pump, an artesian well. People were amazed when that happened. I was amazed too. I irrigate my land from that spring, and my wife sells the vegetables for a good profit. We built a brick home with a metal roof. My wife is healthy, and it is hard for us to believe sometimes that we have been blessed with such abundance in such a short time. We've only known the Lord ten years.

I am not ashamed anymore. Even after I became a Christian, I felt shame for a long while. But I've come to understand that the things I did, I did in ignorance. Though I hurt many people and hurt myself as well, the Lord has given me a second chance. I can never repay him for what He has done for me. I can only do the best I can to serve Him.

I have looked into the jaws of death. I have seen death. And I have been spared, not only from death, but also from hell.

"But my righteousness
will last forever.
My salvation will continue
from generation to generation."
Isaiah 51:8 NLT

THE TIGER LADY

Bev

When the government set the Tharu free from their bond-servant agreements in 2001, many of them had nowhere to go. The government gave them jungle lands and installed a few wells. The Tharu hacked out an existence there, bit by bit, macheting the underbrush and building tiny huts.

Their villages were ramshackle. The people found work in agriculture for meager wages, and they slowly created new lives. The instant mass exodus of twenty-eight thousand slaves put a strain on the countryside, and the people were hopeful but unprepared for instant freedom. The jungles they migrated to were wild.

Share your food with the hungry, and give shelter to the homeless. Give clothes to those who need them, and do not hide from relatives who need your help. Isaiah 58:7

Twilight is beautiful in the jungle. Hazy blues and greens filter golden streaks of sunlight. In October the smoke from burning the fields after harvest makes a fog and a pleasant smell.

The mother hummed as she walked the small dirt path. She made her way, with her two boys, towards the well nearest her hut. She needed water for cooking the family's dinner that night. And she needed a bath. But more than that, her two dirty sons needed a bath. She'd asked them to go with her to carry the bucket, but she had plans of dousing them once they reached the water. One was five years old and the other ten, neither old enough to want to smell nice for a girl. Until then, she'd have to force them to bathe.

The boys took turns tossing a stick to each other all along the ten-minute walk. Finally, it went off the path into the thick of the jungle and they sulked. *As if there are not plenty of other sticks*, she thought. But she let them be. Soon the younger son found another branch and tossed it. The older boy angered when the stick hit him. She saw the fight coming.

"Stop!" she said to her oldest.

He did not stop, and he made a move to punch the younger boy's arm.

"That's it. Now you're both getting a bath." She was pleased with her ingenuity.

They both looked at her, betrayal plain on their faces.

She shrugged. "You did not listen."

They reached the well, and she began to draw water with the bucket. The boys stripped down, and she poured a bucket over each, pointing to the scabbed dirt patches they were to scrub. When they finished, she washed her hands and feet and prepared the bucket she would take back with her. It was a pleasant evening. The air was cooling into fall and not so dank and still as September had been. She smelled food from the surrounding cook fires, and her stomach rumbled. Her husband had brought home a gourd, and she would roast it and add it to their rice.

Her younger son found another stick and started to toss it to his brother. "No," she said. "Get in front of me. Sunila, get behind me." They needed to get home. The sun was setting, and the jungle was darkening around the path. Her younger son started to run ahead, and she chased him for a moment.

From behind her she heard a scream. She turned, and her oldest son had vanished off the path. "Mom! Help!" From deep in the jungle, he called her name. She caught a flash of green and gold in a final streak of sunlight—large, round, shimmering eyes—and her son's bright T-shirt just below them. It turned broadside to run into the jungle, and the last few hints of twilight glowed off the giant beast's orange-and-black striped coat.

From her belly ripped a wail, an animal sound she wasn't sure she had made. She was gripping her younger son's arm, and she didn't know whether to run after the tiger and risk the small child, or stay and keep him safe. Within a minute villagers appeared through the bush. She told them about the tiger, and everyone ran into the dark, thick jungle with sticks, screaming and looking for the boy.

Back in his home in a neighboring settlement, Ganga, a local pastor, had heard the scream. He didn't know what happened, but he grabbed his new motorcycle—the only thing with an electric light for miles around—and he rode in the direction of the scream. When Ganga arrived, he shined the light into the jungle and they found the tiger. It had the boy by the throat. The people united to chase the tiger and it vanished, leaving the boy behind.

Ganga ran to the body, and the boy was still breathing. The mother picked him up and climbed onto the back of Ganga's motorcycle. They drove to the nearest clinic, but by the time they arrived, the boy had died. The tiger had broken his neck and crushed his windpipe. Ganga drove them both home again, the boy's dead body pressed between them on the seat. She wanted to bury him the next day in a peaceful place where she could visit him.

The Tharu knew tigers return later to their kill. That night they put the boy's body in a hut and built a huge campfire near it. Everyone gathered their farming tools and spears, and they sat around the fire, protecting each other, guarding the body, and mourning with the mother. The next day, she put her oldest son in a hole her husband dug, and she covered him in dirt and put golden mums on the fresh, smooth pile of earth. They had a traditional funeral, and people from surrounding villages came to help bury the boy and comfort the family. Everyone was broken and afraid. The sun set again, another twilight, and the mother watched it through the door of her hut from her rope bed, the dirt floor beneath her turning to mud from her tears.

A vehicle rumbled into the village the next morning; she was still on her cot. A shadow appeared in her door. Ganga came in. "I have visitors to see you," he said. She sat up. She felt nothing. She'd not eaten, and her hair was starting to mat. She walked outside, and a group was standing in the middle of the dirt road. They were from a local Nepalgunj church, and KB and Sushila were the leaders. They told her they would build her a well near her house so she wouldn't have to revisit the place where her son was taken. They also promised to install six other wells nearby. They gave her food and gifts. They hugged her and promised to return and help. They prayed with people that day to comfort them, and a few villagers became Christians.

Over the next few months, the vehicle came back many times. Pastors KB and Sushila helped the community learn to farm their own vegetables and collect the seeds for the following year's planting. They taught hygiene and food and water sanitation. They organized the large smattering of huts into separate village groups and taught them how to gather money for a micro-loan program.

Each villager brought ten rupees (about ten cents) a week to their village group "bank," where they deposited the funds into a joint savings account. That account was for village use, for the greater good. If someone needed a taxi ride to the hospital and they could not afford it, it would come from the fund. If someone had a business idea that would benefit the village, like purchasing a share-able piece of farming equipment, five leaders would gather to decide the terms of use. If the vote was unanimous, they would approve the idea and use the money. KB and Sushila's church matched the villagers' giving, rupee for rupee. In the ten years since they instituted this principle, Ganga's village has saved more than twelve thousand dollars.

Within these settlement groups, everyone lives together in peace—Muslim, Hindu, Animist, Christian. They help each other and look out for each other's children. They share food in tough winters. Despite the church being involved and helping these villagers flourish and become self-sustaining farmers, most of them have not converted to Christianity. KB and Sushila do not push them. Most of these people are an hour from the main church building. They will never be tithing members, never serve as greeters or child-care workers. They can never repay what KB, Sushila, and Ganga have done for them.

KB doesn't care about that. "Mourn with those

who mourn," he says, "without an agenda. They can give nothing to us. And that's the point. I am a Christian, but I am also a father and grandfather. I know what it is like to hold a child in my arms. I also know what it is to hold a dying person."

A few years ago, KB was walking down the street when he heard a man screaming. He rushed over to a horse-drawn cart where a man he had gone to school with was lying. A rabid cat had bitten him a month before, and the man was in the final stages of death. Rabies causes a fear of water, and it had started to rain. The man was terrified, shaking. "Everyone was afraid to touch him," KB says. "But I was moved with compassion. To be abandoned like that in the last moments . . . like an animal."

KB, to the crowd's horror, walked over to the man and picked him up; he held the rabid man, carrying him to a dry place. As soon as KB reached a place to lay him, the man died. "Too many people are fighting. And too many are withholding help and goods, loving touch and kindness, because they are too busy disagreeing. We will not do that. The need is too great," KB says.

The lady who lost her son to a tiger is not a Christian, but she is friends with the local pastor, and she loves KB and Sushila. It has been ten years since her son died, ten years since her greatest pain, and ten years since her village began to work together in true community—differences aside.

"When you hear a scream, you run into the jungle with your neighbors; you don't wait in your hut. You run into the dark and you help," KB says. "That's all we are trying to do—run into the dark and help."

Your name, O Lord, endures forever;
your fame, O Lord,
is known to every generation.
Psalms 135:13 NLT

BAJARNI

Rick

I've traveled in nearly fifty countries and lived much of my life among the world's poor. I've eaten their spicy food, slept in their simple homes, journeyed in their rickety buses, shared their sorrows and their celebrations. I've found their faith is not as simple as we like to think. They live in complicated, vulnerable worlds where faith is the only thing that keeps them.

We may think the poor admire us, but that's not always true. Sometimes they feel sorry for us. Sometimes they are ashamed of us. It's difficult for them to understand our waste, our weakness, our petty lives, and our lack of gratitude.

When I speak in their churches, I often ask them to pray for me. I respect their faith. I bow my head and listen, and honor their tears with my own. Their prayers have produced tangible results in my life. They see things differently, from a spiritual perspective, and their faith operates in a different arena. In many ways, they bring a slice of Peter into my life: "I don't have any silver or gold for you. But I'll give you what I have. In the name of Jesus Christ the Nazarene, get up and walk!" (Act 3:6 NLT).

The Lord is close to the broken-
hearted; he rescues those
whose spirits are crushed.
Psalm 34:18 NLT

She is not shy; she seems unshakable. Her skin is warm burnt sienna. It is smooth, which makes her look young, but she is a grandmother with four children. She looks tired, or more like she's lived many lives, a little serious, driven by something internal. She is a machine—determined, stubborn, persistent.

Her clothes don't match; they don't have to. Matching is impractical. Her shirt is gray and gauzy, but not the gauze of fine fabric, the gauze of poor thread count. Her head covering is peach with lavender flowers. Her skirt is sky-blue paisley, the color of a water-park slide, and it has thick red horizontal stripes.

Her face is small and rectangular with a strong, smooth jaw and a parrot mouth protruding just beyond her elegant nose, then slipping back into a delicate chin. When she smiles, her mouth spreads thin across her square teeth in a perfect oval, displaying both top and bottom rows.

Her hands are tiny and covered with black rectangular tattoos in crude rows. Only her palms are free of marks. Her nails are short black rims of dirt wedged under the rounded crescents. She tells her story in a tiny voice—tiny, but not fearful or shy. She speaks in Tharu, which is translated to Nepali, then to English.

She was a villager, and though she was superstitious and uneducated, she was a Brahmin, a woman of status. The lower castes existed to serve her. They labored for their Hindu masters, the landowners and the haughty priests of a five-thousand-year-old organized religion. Everyone held a predetermined rank in this remnant of Mesopotamia.

Most of the Christians were descendants of the untouchables, so unclean to the pious elites that they could not draw water from the same well or meet the gaze of the upper castes or pollute them by their presence. They were still untouchable as far as she was concerned.

The British had changed much of the caste system in India, and when India gained her independence in 1947, the new democracy continued to make reluctant concessions to the lower castes. But the British never conquered Nepal. Change, in that fiercely independent zone between India and China, came much more slowly.

She had been a sickly child, and her father, though he was a guru, could not heal her. Her family had wasted most of their livelihood seeking to help her. They had given thousands of rupees to gurus for animal sacrifices and for offerings to the idols.

They had taken her to hospitals and local clinics, but nothing helped. She had become so weak that she was confined to her bed and eventually paralyzed through inactivity. She began having seizures.

Christians had visited her, telling her that Jesus could heal her, but she would not listen to them. She told her relatives to chase them away. Christianity was for the lower castes, the cow eaters. She would not stoop to associate with them.

She grew up in a magical world between heaven and earth: a world where the spirits are just as real as people, a world of sorcery and fortune telling and gurus. She was alive to that world, reading cryptic messages in the insect-like song of a grass warbler, the appearance of a snake at the edge of the village, or an early monsoon rain. She knew how to divine an egg yolk and how to read a palm. Her father taught her those things. She could hear the whispers of the spirit world. But she could not heal herself, and neither could her father.

Her husband was an adulterer and an alcoholic. When they sold their rice at harvest, he would give the money to women and to his friends, then come home drunk and beat her until he passed out from exhaustion. Her father-in-law said he was worthless. She hated him. She hated everyone. She hated her life.

She was angry—angry, and hurt, and wounded. The anger festered within her until it consumed her. Her illness deepened and became, not just the illness of a broken body, but the illness of a tormented mind and a tortured heart, as if her spirit had followed her sickly body down into the bowels of hell. She fought with everyone: her neighbors, her family, her friends. She sat in the dark inner room of her home, and she seethed.

Her father sent her to live with a guru more powerful than he. She lived with him for six months, and she improved. She reached the point where she could cook and clean and serve him, but if she left him, her sickness would return. Though the seizures stopped and she regained her strength, she was trapped in servitude. At least it was a better life than what she had before.

She traveled with the old guru to Nepalgunj and visited her sister who was living there. Her sister had become a Christian, which bewildered her, but her sister seemed happy. "Why don't you come to the church with me?" her sister asked.

"I suppose I've nothing to lose," she said.

She walked down the narrow lane to the church as if in a trance, but at the gate she felt something. People were singing inside, their harmony unlike anything she had heard before. They were clapping their hands, and their sound was joyful, like a wedding celebration. They did not sing in the monotonous chants of the Hindus. Their music was more complicated, more expressive, more hopeful—as if they knew the gods were pleased with them.

The moment she entered the compound gate, she began weeping. She wept through the service, and at the end she could hardly speak to the kind lady who seemed to be in charge.

"Why don't you sleep here?" the lady asked.

"Yes," she said, "I think I will sleep here. It is peaceful."

The lady brought her some tea and something to eat, a little rice and dal and cauliflower, and she lay down on a mat on the church floor. There were other churchwomen who slept there with her while the men slept in a nearby school.

In the night a man came to her in a dream. He wore a dazzling white robe, and his face and hair shone as if lit from within. He was the most beautiful man she had ever seen, kind, attentive, intelligent. She thought he was a guru, and she held her palm out to him for a reading.

He did not take her palm but smiled and said, "I have brought you from death to life."

That was all he said. He did not tell her his name or where he came from or what he wanted of her. She did not know who he was until later when she told her dream to the women who had slept with her on the church floor. She had seen the Lord.

The women taught her how to pray, how to worship, and how to sing the Christian songs. They gave her a New Testament. She had difficulty understanding the things she read in the little book, but she understood the kindness and the love the women gave her.

After three days she returned to her village but soon fell ill, even worse than before. She did not understand why, but she had never felt better than when she was with the church people. She told her family to take her back to Nepalgunj, and she stayed with the believers for two weeks. After those two weeks, she was never sick again.

Her return to her village was not an easy one. Some of the villagers were amazed at her recovery, and many of them became believers, too. But the gurus were angry. They stood against her, using abusive language and threatening her. They told her that if anyone died in the village, they would bury that person in her home. They spoke mantras[33] against her and cursed her before the villagers.

The first time she saw the fire come against her, it frightened her. It came in the evening while she sat on her porch drinking a cup of tea. She told herself, *This is not a real fire.* She knew when she saw it that it was not real. It was a ghost of a fire, but it was terrifying, as frightening as the wildfire she had once seen racing through the dry rice chaff of a late harvest.

It came with the sound of a strong wind, rolling across the rice field adjacent to her property. She froze, her hand trembling, the tea sloshing from the cup and staining her sari. The fire roared up to the threshold of her home, then suddenly quenched. As quickly as it had come, it died. A week later it came again, rushing into her bedroom as she slept. She awoke with a start to see it die at the foot of her bed.

For several months the ghost fire would come, sometimes in the day, but usually in the night or early morning. Then, after a long while, a guru visited her.

"We performed many mantras against you," he said. "But your religion is a true religion. We see that there is nothing we can do to stop you."

She finishes her story and is quiet, her hands folded meekly in her lap. She seems preoccupied with a thought, so I wait, watching her, not saying anything. She gazes into the distance with the serenity of someone who has made peace with herself and with her enemy. She is no longer angry or wounded or combative. Her husband has passed away, but he made things right with her before he departed. He came to the Lord and to his senses. He repented to her, and he told her he was sorry.

She sits still, gazing toward the horizon through clear, unwavering dark eyes. She is quiet—one of those people who is not intimidated by silent moments. Her breathing is shallow and steady and strong. She has that otherworldly look about her, as if she is expecting something, or perhaps someone.

I recognize that look. It is the look of someone who is in love. It is the look of someone who expects the return of a beautiful man she met long ago in a dream—a man who gazed into her soul with kindness and grace and mercy.

*Let each generation
tell its children of your mighty acts;
let them proclaim your power.*
Psalms 145:4 NLT

GOVINDA

Rick

God blesses those who are humble,
for they will inherit the whole earth.
Matthew 5:5 NLT

I've known Govinda since he was a teen. He's one of those quiet, unassuming guys who are easy to underestimate. He is not lean, like most of the young men from the villages, but a little pudgy; not overweight, but soft, with a round, serene Buddha face. Like many of the Tharu leaders, he weeps when he prays, and he approaches me with an almost embarrassing reverence.

I've always appreciated the way the Asians honor their elders, but among the Hindu converts, the devotion to pastors can be a little unsettling. I think it comes from their religious background. The Hindus worship their gurus as if they are gods. Respect is important in their world, and the gurus love their status. They often look haughty. Like the Scribes and Pharisees of Jesus' day, they seem to enjoy the fawning their followers give them when they touch their feet and shower them with jasmine petals or place chrysanthemum garlands around their necks.

That's the thing about first-generation believers.

They bring customs into their faith that may be foreign to us. Some of those practices are healthy, some
maybe not. I don't care for the excessive honor they
sometimes give me, but I admire their humility and
their modesty. That modesty is more Hindu than
it is Christian, at least in the Christianity that most
of us know. I often find myself apologizing for the
dress and behavior of the freewheeling Westerners
who visit our work. And though I'm grateful for the
access that the westernization of South Asia has
given me, I regret the Nepalis' lost innocence. Our
free way of life is a wonderful thing, but it comes
with some baggage.

We have a cup of tea together, and I congrat-
ulate Govinda on his recent marriage. His wife is
a delightful girl, quiet, attractive, and respectful,
just like Govinda. They seem well suited for each
other, and I imagine that they will have a good life
together. Neither of them likes to travel. They're
homebodies—with the perfect pastor personality:
patient, kind, thoughtful, instantly likable.

"Your mom told me you were a good child," I
say. "She says you did housework for her, even as
a little boy, and that you became a believer early in
life. That you were not spoiled by the world."

He smiles and is quiet for a moment. He is so

much like his mom Bajarni, reflective, soft-spoken. He always pauses before he speaks, sometimes for a long while, but when he speaks, he is clear, his thoughts well formed.

"I was a fearful child, but any child would have been fearful in that home. The shouting, the fights, and the bickering made for an unpredictable life, especially to a little one. At a time when I needed to feel safe, I was not at all safe. I never knew when my father would come home to disrupt an already unstable life with his raging.

"I learned to watch my mother carefully, and from an early age, I could discern her mood. If she cradled her tea in both hands and held the cup near her face to savor the scent, it would be a pleasant day. She would not scream at me, and if I were good and helped with the chores, she would sit with me and caress the side of my face, and tell me that I was a good boy.

"If she drank her tea hurriedly, it would be an angry day. She would shout at me and berate me. There would be no pleasing her, no matter how hard I worked to clean and cook and gather firewood.

"If she set her tea down half-finished and neglected it until it grew cold, it would be a dark day. She would speak hardly a word. There would be no cuddling in the evening, and there would be no meal unless I cooked it. She would brood through the day on her bed. She would draw tight the curtain that separated the bed from the rest of the common family room, and I would not see her until the next day. At times she remained there two days. When that darkness settled over her, she would not eat or speak. Sometimes I would bring her a little plate of dal and rice or a boiled egg, but she usually left the food untouched.

"I stuttered. I quit school because of the stuttering. It was impossible. If the teacher asked me a question, I would freeze, and try as I may, the words would not come. I could see the words in my head, but they would not come out. I would try to think of synonyms, but those words wouldn't come out either. More words would come, and I would get so confused in my mind that I could not choose which one to say. And in the back of the class, a girl would snicker or a boy would whisper, '*Dht, dht, dht,*' and I would shut down. I would stare down at my desk until the teacher grew impatient and asked her question to another child."

"You don't stutter now," I say. "In fact, you are very well spoken, and you're a pastor. You have a big church. How did you overcome it?"

"Moses stuttered, too," he says with a little smile. "I was thirteen when I followed Christ. My mother had been a Christian for about a month, and I wanted to be like her. She changed so much and so quickly, I knew that it was real.

"Nothing happened when she prayed for my healing. I went back to school, but I continued to struggle. The kids still made fun of me because of my speech, but now they also persecuted me because I was a Christian. It was even worse than before. I managed to make it to the tenth grade, but I finally dropped out. It was too much.

"I lived a normal Christian life for about five years. My mother gave me a New Testament, and I read it constantly. The more I read and the more I thought about the healing stories in the Bible, the more my faith grew. After a few years, my speech improved and I could speak clearly.

"There were only a few believers in my village. Many people believed that Jesus had healed my mom, and they would even come to her for prayer; very few of them became Christians. There was no one to lead us.

"When I was about eighteen, the believers who met in my mother's home to pray asked me to become their pastor. I told them I could not, that I was too young and I didn't know how to lead them. But one afternoon while I was taking a nap, I dreamed of Jesus on the cross. From that day on, I told the Lord I would serve Him."

"I'm curious about why the village people would come to your mother for prayer, but they would not follow the Lord," I say. "They all believed that the Lord had healed your mom. How is it that they believe in His power to heal, but they will not become Christians?"

"It's because of the persecution," he says. "It is very difficult to follow the Lord in these villages. It's not like your country. Here, Christians are cut off from their families. They lose their inheritance. How can you live if you have no land?

"If you are a young girl, no one will marry you. If you are a married woman, your husband will not allow you to become a Christian. If you are a man, no one will do business with you or trade with you or help you. People will ridicule you in public, and if anything bad happens in the village, they will blame you. They will say you have made the gods angry and brought a curse on the village. Just recently some Hindu men in India cornered one of our pastors. They spat on the ground and made him lick it up. It humiliated him, but they would have beaten him otherwise.

"Sometimes we pray for people and they receive a miracle, and yet they will not follow the Lord. They believe that Jesus is a healer, but they have difficulty accepting Him as the one Lord.

"There was a man in Sovangar who got sick. A man in his village told his wife if she would take him to the church, the Christians would pray for him and he would live. He was too sick to travel, so she came to us and begged us to come pray for him. I took some brothers with me and we rode our bicycles there, but it took us most of the day to reach his home. By the time we reached there, he had died. The villagers had taken him to the hospital, and the doctor had pronounced him dead. They were about to take him for cremation.

"We thought, 'What can we do now? He is dead; there is no pulse, no breath, he is cold.' We decided that since we had come so far, we would pray anyway. We prayed for about three hours, and he began breathing. And after a short time, he started walking around.

"He kept saying, 'God is real! God is real!' And many people came to the Lord. About forty people were there when that happened; all of them became believers. We started a church there. After two years he quit following the Lord. Only four or five of those forty people are still Christians. They could not stand the persecution."

"How can that be?" I ask. "I find this hard to believe. The man died. They all saw it. How can they not continue in their faith?"

"It's like the rich man and Lazarus," Govinda says. "The rich man, who had died and was in hell, asked Abraham to send Lazarus to his father's home to warn his five brothers of the torment. Abraham told him: 'Moses and the prophets have warned them. Your brothers can read what they wrote. The rich man replied, "No, Father Abraham! But if someone is sent to them from the dead, then they will repent of their sins and turn to God." But Abraham said, "If they won't listen to Moses and the prophets, they won't be persuaded even if someone rises from the dead"'" (Luke 16:29–31 NLT).

I have difficulty with this, and I say again, "Govinda, this just can't be. The man was dead! How can he not follow the Lord?"

Govinda pauses for a long while, his gaze fastened on the floor. Then, with a sigh, he raises his head and looks me straight in the eye. "I don't know, Pastor. It is difficult for us to understand, too. The enemy is strong in his deception.

"A little five-year-old girl in this very village was also raised from the dead. Her grandfather was a guru. She fell sick and he performed mantras over her for a week, but she died. The grandfather pronounced her dead, and they were taking her for burial. We went there and caught them along the way. We anointed her with oil and prayed for her, and in a short time she awoke and sat up. Not many days later, the grandfather died. The girl is fourteen now, and she has been faithful to the Lord. All of her family members are believers. We have seen many miracles among the Tharu, but these two are the most notable."

My tea has grown cold, and I toss it into the nearby ferns. It is warm, and we have been sitting outside, cross-legged on a wooden rope bed under the cover of a fig tree. They grow big here, and this one provides deep shade for the courtyard of the Tharu home we are staying in. The women have a fire going in the open kitchen, and the sun will soon set. They have just started the curry and have thrown leeks, garlic, ghee, and a handful of masala into a large pot. A sharp sizzle and a promising aroma waft out over the courtyard. We all take note, glancing toward the kitchen, each of us estimating how long it will be until dinner. From the other side of the back wall of the kitchen, I hear the squawk of a chicken and the thud of an axe on a wooden block. *About ninety minutes,* I think. It is a little late for tea, but the kettle is still on the fire, so I ask for another cup.

I sit for a long while, sipping that hot, sweet tea, trying my best to figure it out. Like Govinda says, "It is difficult to understand."

I've been just about everywhere on this planet. I've pretty much heard it all. When I hear stories like this, I struggle. Sometimes they just don't make sense. Why would the guru grandfather die after his granddaughter was raised from the dead, or at the least, out of a coma? Did he reject the Lord's mercy? Was he that stubborn in his traditions? And why would he do that? He witnessed, firsthand, a rare miracle. Was he angry that he could not heal the child and that the Christians had raised her from the dead? And the man who was raised from the dead—why would he not follow the Lord? It's unfathomable!

Yet the Scriptures describe similar scenarios. There were ten lepers whom Jesus healed, but only one returned to thank Him. Ten were healed, but only one became a follower. And when Jesus raised Lazarus from the dead, the Bible says that "many of the people who were with Mary believed in Jesus when they saw this happen. But some went to the Pharisees and told them what Jesus had done" (John 11:45–46 NLT). Even the most notable miracle Jesus performed brought division. Some believed and followed Him, but some were threatened in their traditions and went straight to Jesus' persecutors.

In non-Christian cultures, the wealthy and the powerful have the most to lose. The gospel threatens their status and their economic systems. Those systems are perpetuated through religion, social pressure, politics, and financial leverage. It usually doesn't take long for the powerful to recognize that the gospel dismantles those prejudicial systems. They will fight it, and they will incite opposition.

When Paul, in Acts 19, was preaching in Ephesus, a wealthy silversmith named Demetrius recognized the threat the gospel posed to his tidy religious enterprise, so he organized a riot opposing Paul. He even admitted his motivation when he said to his peers, "Gentlemen, you know that our wealth comes from this business. But as you have seen and heard, this man Paul has persuaded many people that handmade gods aren't really gods at all" (Acts 19:25–26 NLT).

Sometimes miracles are not enough to persuade people to follow Christ. Followers are not made through miracles. They may be attracted through miracles and convinced of the reality of Christ through miracles, but followers are built through conviction, through repentance, and through faith.

Even the Pharisees did not doubt Jesus' miracles: "Then the leading priests and Pharisees called the high council together. 'What are we going to do?' they asked each other. 'This man certainly performs many miraculous signs. If we allow him to go on like this, soon everyone will believe in him. Then the Roman army will come and destroy both our Temple and our nation'" (John 11:47–48 NLT).

The Pharisees understood that they were in an ideological conflict. They were caught between the powerful Roman political system and the enterprising Jewish religious system. To continue reaping the financial advantages those two systems gave them, they could not allow any changes in the status quo. It did not matter if Jesus was teaching truth or performing miracles. They had to resist change at all costs in order to maintain their advantage.

They also understood that they were in a war. In war there are those who form the support and those who fight. The support apparatus is usually the most costly and complicated structure in the war effort. It is where most of the manpower is concentrated, and it is the place where most of the resources are used. In religious systems the elite do not fight, but they do often incite violence through inflammatory rhetoric. This was the case in Jesus' time, and it is still the case in regions like South Asia where Christianity represents a threat to the Hindu political, cultural, and religious systems. They don't doubt miracles; they are threatened by them.

Westerners often doubt miracles. We struggle to accept that the Lord still performs them. We often attribute miracles to superstition, gullibility, or perhaps to chance. But on the front lines of the gospel's advance, the authenticity of miracles is seldom challenged. In fact, both the believers and the unbelievers accept miracles. But as it was in the time of Christ, miracles, even the most notable ones, do not always convince people to follow the Lord.

*Your faithfulness extends
to every generation,
as enduring as the earth you created.*
Psalms 119:90 NLT

SUE

Bev

The angel of the LORD found Hagar
near a spring in the desert. . . .
He said, "Where have you come from,
and where are you going? . . .
I will increase your descendants
so much that they will be
too numerous to count." . . .
She gave this name to the LORD
who spoke to her:
"You are the God who sees me,"
for she said, "I have now seen
the One who sees me."
Genesis 16:7–8; 10; 13 NIV

Sue had a strong British accent. I tried to think of her making scones and clotted cream, shooing sheep from the front door of her little house in Nottingham, England. We sat next to each other at dinner in Nepal, a jumble of Americans, Europeans, Indians, and Nepalis. She wore an emerald sari, bedecked with hand-sewn sequins and jewels. A sari wraps around the hips twice, puckering in beautiful pleats and covering a long petticoat, then sweeps up over the shoulder. The long elegant dress is tight around the bottom and leaves the stomach exposed—lumpy, pregnant, concave from hunger, sculpted, or muscular—nobody cares about that sort of thing in Nepal. Sue is queenly in her sari, and I tell her so.

"Ah, but I feel a bit dumpy at home in England. I wear slacks and a shirt, and you know, it doesn't suit. Saris are for everyone." She smiles at me. She is six feet tall with a choppy gray pixie cut. She wears thick-framed black glasses that give one the appearance of being looked at from the other end of a microscope. She turns to a girl next to us at the table and orders her dinner in fluent Nepali.

I ask how long she has been in the country. "Eighteen years now," she replies. At first glance I thought she was *that* kind of tourist—the kind who goes in search of herself in an ashram in the East, gets straight off the plane and buys a sari from an airport shop. But on closer inspection, her sari is older, with gently worn seams. It is well cared for and obviously loved.

"It was time to move on from Bangladesh," she says. She tears a piece of roti and scoops up some rice with it. She eats with her hands, like a Nepali. "I was there for two years before I came here," she says. "I'm a teacher."

She was only nineteen when she knew she wanted to be a teacher overseas. Sue led her local

Christian student union during college, and she felt certain she wanted to be a missionary teacher. "But I went to Overseas Volunteer Services and they turned me down flat. So I thought, *Well, it's not that then.*"

She'd lived a sheltered life. "At that point I'd never been outside of England. I went to a teachers' training college in Retford. It was very small. And I grew up in a fishing village called Brixham."

She graduated college and settled into workaday life, teaching in a Catholic school. She met a local businessman, and after a year of dating, they married. Two kids later, she was a schoolteacher and church volunteer, in an unhappy marriage.

"Even in those first two years of marriage, I thought I'd wrecked my opportunity to go overseas. I walked away from God because of it. That closeness had gone, and it was awful. I'd go out with friends, and I'd sit there thinking I wasn't having any fun. They were all desperately chasing drink, trying to enjoy themselves, and I knew the real enjoyment was with God."

She says the first crack in the marriage appeared when she wanted to be in church instead of a pub. Diving headlong into church, she volunteered for the boys' club, girls' club, youth group. Between her teaching full-time and church work, her husband felt ignored. They divorced in the nineties after more than two decades of marriage. Sue sent her boys to college, saw them begin to succeed on their own, and decided it was time for a life change.

The opportunity came when her school down-sized and merged with another district. She went to a job fair, and in little print in the *Nottingham Teacher's Circular*, she saw an advertisement for a teacher's job in Bangladesh and decided to apply for it. It was the only job she could find that didn't require Bible college.

"On my application, I still couldn't say I'd traveled much." She'd only been to Sweden for three days with her ex-husband and to Spain once for a holiday. She went to her town library and found a map and located Bangladesh. Then she went to the travel-book section and borrowed the only book on Bangladesh, full of warnings to female visitors.

She got the job and moved to Bangladesh. After two years she moved to Nepal, working as a school-teacher and eventually as principal in a mission school. As she taught, she started to notice a trend. Nepali kids, if they went to school at all, only stayed until they were eight; then they were needed for their families' farms. The girls didn't usually attend school at all. I ask what the attendance rate was.

"Oh, zero percent past eight, when I first started the program," she says.

"And now?"

"Ninety percent."

But that success didn't happen overnight. She was working for a Christian social-welfare organiza-tion, running their mission school, when she started an NGO for Nepali kids. Sue has to deal with new visas every year, resettling with the government to allow her to stay. She travels home and to different churches to speak and raise funds for herself and others in her nonprofit. She battles old mind-sets about education.

"They only learn by rote—just basic memorization. I attended a village meeting one time when the parents said their children knew their numbers and letters, and that their kids wouldn't be attending school any longer. They knew the numbers, but they couldn't apply the knowledge. I asked the kids to count to ten in front of the parents and teachers. They counted. Then I asked them to go outside and each bring me seven rocks. Only one student could do it. Well, I had their attention then. They let me do what I needed to do."

Sue began teaching teachers how to teach. She showed them that teaching the children *how* to think, not just *what* to think, was important. She was so successful in teaching applied education that children began reading loan paperwork and showing their illiterate parents where moneylenders had scammed them.

She says she's got to go home to England in December, and I ask if she's tired. I know I would be.

"Heavens, no. My visa is expiring through my nonprofit, and they told me in June that there are young people coming up who know how to use a computer who will take my place." She handles the conversation with grace. "One young girl came to teach, but she only lasted six months. She couldn't handle the solitude, the quiet contemplation. Not many of them last reading by candlelight during a rolling blackout. Most can't survive without their Internet. It's quite a learning curve."

Sue even stayed during the Maoist rebellion, the civil war that shook Nepal. Many with a non-Nepali passport were on a plane as fast as possible, but she couldn't leave what had become her home, even if she had citizenship and a pastoral English countryside home waiting for her. "I recall walking home one day, and I stopped in at a friend's house. Just moments later, a bomb went off where I would have been walking. So we just locked her doors and windows and made tea. We hunkered down on the floor and listened to the bullets whizzing by and talked about our day. I stayed an hour later than I would have that evening, just to be safe."

She says this with such serenity. She is like a monk, someone forged in the depths of solitude. It's not just that she's an introvert, gone inside herself to find solace. Her peace exudes out of her—she's made a hula-hoop–sized bubble of calm around her. The room we are in smells of tea. The fan is gentle. It feels a bit like a psychiatrist's office—that medical quiet, a purposeful pause. I ask if she has any regrets.

"No. Only that I worked too much in church

before I went. I gave so much, and it was a little bit of striving on my part, you know, because I was trying to fill that hole. I knew I wanted to be a missionary, and I'd thought I'd ruined it. But here I am." She looks down and smooths her sari. She's nodding to herself. "I've already told God I want to die with my boots on, heading to one place or another."

I tell her I'm curious what the people at home thought about her leaving that first time.

"Well, they were nervous, you know. The church thought I was crazy. Me, forty-seven years old then and only been to Sweden. They thought it was a midlife crisis."

"Right. Like, 'Sue, just dye your hair or buy a sports car. There are easier ways to have a midlife,'" I tell her.

"They told me I was being unwise, not thinking about my future. The pastor said he needed me in the church for the youth program I was in charge of then. Yet . . . someone stepped up when I left."

"And how many children's lives have you changed in Nepal since you've arrived?" I ask.

"Oh, about twelve thousand."

*Generations come
and generations go,
but the earth never changes.*
Ecclesiastes 1:4

Acknowledgments

Thanks to Kirby Carol who contributed to this project, to Brenda Pitts for editing, to KB and Sushilla Basel for their deep and enduring friendship, to David Knox for introducing us to KB, and thanks especially to the amazing Nepali believers.

END NOTES

1 **Cow dung** – Cow and buffalo dung will dry to a hard glaze when spread over a mud floor or on mud walls. It's a common practice among tribal people around the world, especially in Africa and South Asia. Researchers at the University of Bristol in the United Kingdom have discovered that the bacteria *mycobacterium vaccae*, found in cow dung, activates a group of neurons in the brain that produces serotonin, a hormone that contributes to feelings of wellbeing and contentedness. Other studies have discovered cow dung to be a natural disinfectant, an insect repellent, and an insulating barrier.

2 **KB and Sushila Basel** – Bev and I were introduced to KB and Sushila through a friend, Pastor David Knox. When we met KB, he was pastoring a main congregation of about 150 adults and had established around twenty village churches. Though their work was small at that time, their leadership potential was obvious. Bev and I worked actively with them, spending three to six months of each year in Nepalgunj, Nepal. In about ten years' time, we were able to help them expand their ministry to over three hundred churches, representing about twenty thousand people as of early 2017.

3 **Jacob and Esau** – Jacob came from a rather dysfunctional family. He was his mother's favorite, a homebody, quiet, and apparently rather hairless, at

least compared to his older brother, Esau. The Bible doesn't really say, but from what it implies, Jacob may not have been a model of masculinity, though he was definitely a man who interested the Lord.

4 **Gurkha** – The British, in colonial times, never conquered Nepal. The Gurkhas were the reason. They were a fearless warrior caste, and they were never subjugated. The British were so impressed that they recruited them as mercenaries. They served in the East India Company army, the British Indian army, and later in World War II in the British army. Today they are commonly employed in security units across Asia, serving a wide array of embassies, including the United States Navy.

5 **Indradrev** – Pastor Indradrev is now married and recently completed the construction of a five-hundred-seat building. His main congregation has around four hundred adults, and he has a vision to expand that church to a thousand members. He oversees an expanding group of about twelve churches representing approximately 1,500 believers.

6 **Royal Family of Nepal** – Until 2008, Nepal was the world's only Hindu kingdom. King Gyanendra was Nepal's last monarch. His reign began in June 2001 after Crown Prince Nependra murdered ten members of the royal family. The tragedy rocked Nepal and contributed to a decade of political chaos. In mid-June of that same year, a Hindu ceremony was held to banish Nependra's ghost

from the nation. In 2008, after years of Maoist-led insurgency, the monarchy was suspended as part of a peace deal with the rebel forces. This ended the Shaw dynasty, a monarchy that had unified and ruled Nepal since 1760.

7 **Maoists** – There are two principal streams of Marxism: the Russian Communists, who follow Lenin, and the Chinese Maoists, who follow Mao Zedong. Maoism is a bottom-led rural movement, the peasants being the force of revolution, while Communism is a middle-led urban movement, the working class being the force of revolution. Movements like the Shining Path in Peru, the Nepali Maoists, and the Naxalite of India are rural insurgencies that were influenced but not directly linked to the Chinese form of Marxism.

8 **Dal Bhat** – The national dish of Nepal, dal bhat, a dish of steamed rice and yellow lentils, is very nutritional. Dry dal is 25 percent protein, comparable to meat. Steamed rice provides the amino acids necessary to make the combined dish a complete protein that is low in fat and high in fiber.

9 Joachim Hagopian, Global Human Trafficking, a Modern Form of Slavery

10 Prof. Martin Patt, "Human Trafficking & Modern-day Slavery—Nepal," www.gvnet.com/humantrafficking/Nepal.htm.

11 www.TheRickshawRun.com.

12 Office to Monitor and Combat Trafficking in Persons, 2016 Trafficking Report, www.state.gov/j/

tip/rls/tiprpt/countries/2016/258829.htm.

13 Hazel Thompson, *Taken*, Jubilee Campaign, E-book.

14 Ibid.

15 Christina Hillstrom, "Circus Slaves," *A Creative Commons Attribution* (June 2010), www. humangoods.net http://humangoods.net/?p=644.

16 Suryatapa Bhattacharya, "India Police Probe Trade in Human Organs," *Dow Jones and Company* (June 2016), www.wsj.com.

17 **Honor Killing** – One of the greatest tragedies of South Asia is the barbaric practice of honor killing. The male leaders in medieval, misogynist cultures, which may be Islamic, Hindu, or Buddhist, believe it is their duty to protect the family honor when a woman commits a grievous moral sin or shames the family. Adultery, premarital intimacy, refusal to enter into an arranged marriage, and behavior that shames the family are punishable by death at the hands of the husband, father, or elder brother.

18 **Kukri Knife** – A heavy inward-curving knife peculiar to Nepal. It is used as a weapon and a utility knife for just about everything. Every Nepali man owns one, and every Nepali woman has one in her kitchen.

19 **Khata** – A ceremonial scarf that originated in Tibetan Buddhism and is always given as a welcome or parting gift to a visitor in Nepal. It is made of silk and is usually white or light gold. It symbolizes purity and compassion. Christians often practice

this tradition since it is more cultural than religious.

20 **Aryan** – The Indo-Aryans may have originated in Iran and migrated into the northern regions of the India subcontinent around 1800 BC. They were part of what is known as the Indo-European migrations. There are linguistic, genetic, and cultural similarities that link them to the Middle East and Central Asia.

21 **Terai** – The Terai is the plain of southern Nepal and northern India. It is a rich agricultural area known for its grain production, especially rice. Because it is flat, much of it is susceptible to flooding during the monsoons. It is by far the most heavily populated region of Nepal.

22 **Sanskrit** – The ancient and sacred language text of Hinduism. It is one of the oldest of the Indo-European languages. It is used as a ceremonial language in Hindu religious rituals, classical Hindustani music performances, and classical literature.

23 **Brahmin** – The priestly caste of Hinduism. They are traditionally responsible for religious rituals, temple service, and the study of the Hindu scriptures.

24 **Sundari** – The queen of a group of ten goddesses in Hindu mythology. She is always portrayed as a sixteen-year-old girl, representing the sixteen human desires.

25 **Animal Sacrifice** – A controversial animal sacrifice takes place each year in Nepal on the eighth and ninth day of the fifteen-day Dishain

festival. Tens of thousands of goat, sheep, and water buffalo are ritually sacrificed in Nepal's most important national and religious holiday. In Bhaktapur, an important historical Hindu kingdom city, the blood literally flows in the streets.

26 **Blind Children's Home** – In 2008 I hiked up into the Jumla region where I visited a blind children's home that was supported by a European philanthropy. The conditions were not good. Two years later that organization discontinued their support and I took on the responsibility of caring for seventeen blind children. We eventually purchased property and built a home for them.

27 **Biryani** – A delicious rice dish that is easy to cook for large crowds.

28 Matthew 18:20 NIV

29 **Jaunting Car** – A lightweight cart pulled by a single horse. Balanced on two wheels the cart is precarious, and in the market areas, often overloaded and unbalanced. I've seen horses stumble to their knees under the weight and once saw a small horse dangled several feet off the ground, leveraged by an overloaded cart.

30 **Squatters** – Property ownership in South Asia is complicated. In urban areas property disputes and fraud are common. In the villages property is registered with the government based on boundaries that may go back several generations. The poor oftentimes squat on government land, and though it is illegal, the local governments are usually

sympathetic.

31 O. Henry, "The Gift of the Magi," first published in *The New York Sunday World*, December 10, 1906.

32 **Deus ex Machina** – "God from the machine"; a plot device where an unexpected event abruptly resolves an impossible problem.

33 **Mantra** – From Sanskrit, it is a sacred chant or utterance in Hinduism and Buddhism. It can be in the form of a song, a poem, a repetitive phrase, or even a sound with no literal meaning.

Only the living can praise you
as I do today.
Each generation
tells of your faithfulness
to the next.
Isaiah 38:19 NLT

CPSIA information can be obtained
at www.ICGtesting.com
Printed in the USA
BVHW04s2236190418
513841BV00001B/1/P